"EXCUSES, EXCUSES . . ."

"Excuses, Excuses..."

The essential handbook by
PAUL JAMES

ЯR
Ravette Limited

Printed and bound in Great Britain
for Ravette Limited,
12 Star Road, Partridge Green, Horsham,
Sussex RH13 8RA
by Cox & Wyman Ltd, Reading
Photoset in Century Schoolbook
by JH Graphics Ltd, Reading

ISBN 0 906710 82 0

Dedicated to Karen B
whose excuses were a constant source
of inspiration!

ACKNOWLEDGEMENTS

I would like to thank the following for permission to use copyright material:

Chappell Music Limited London for 'Miss Otis Regrets', words and music by Cole Porter © 1934 Harms Inc.
Duckworth and Company Limited for permission to quote from 'Indian Summer' by Dorothy Parker from 'The Collected Dorothy Parker' © 1973.
The Society of Authors on behalf of the Bernard Shaw Estate for permission to quote from 'Pygmalion' by George Bernard Shaw.
Margaret Ramsay Limited, the Estate of Joe Orton, for permission to quote from 'Entertaining Mr. Sloane' by Joe Orton, published by Eyre Methuen London 1973 © 1964 Joe Orton.

I wish also to express my sincere thanks to: Dr John Edmunds, John Lawton, Joseph Gordon, Alan Howard Evans, Annette Noman and Peter G. Wood for their invaluable help, advice and excuses, and, of course, the inimitable Dame Hilda Bracket for being a constant source of inspiration to us all.

CONTENTS

FOREWORD

by Dame Hilda Bracket

Being asked to write the foreword to this charming book gives me the excuse for saying . . . I never need any excuses! Personally I have no time for people who insist on making excuses every time you meet them. My lifelong friend, Dr Evadne Hinge PTH (one of only three registered part-time herbalists in the country) for instance couldn't get by without them, she has an answer for everything. Frequently she blames her mother, and that woman *has* got a lot to answer for, but more often than not I become the victim of her own inadequacies.

Take the time she told members of the Old Stackton Society that the Doomsday Book was out of print. She only said this because she couldn't remember where she'd put it. And the time she fell downstairs with a pot of herbal tea and said she was only trying to remove a stain on the hall carpet. And the famous time when we were appearing at the Snitterton Empire in a performance of *Götterdämmerung*, Evadne was in the pit conducting from a score of Perchance to Dream. Her excuse that time was that she wanted to see how alert we all were. And how could I ever forget that night in 1951 in that same season at Snitterton (the Empire is now sadly demolished – the following week I think) when I was playing Aida. As we reached the climax of the opera and I was being drawn into the tomb, Evadne pulled the wrong switch, the lights went out and I plummeted feet-first into the orchestra pit. Straight into the brass section. I naturally assumed that she would apologise, but oh no, she claimed that she had dimmed the lights deliberately for dramatic effect, and that it was my own fault for standing too close to the edge of the stage. 'Attack is the best form of defence' has always been Evadne's motto. I haven't been able to look at a French horn since.

Not that I'm one to complain but she has an annoying habit of putting her Wellington boots on the wrong feet and walking out backwards, and then accuses me of walking away from her. I wonder what excuse her father gave to her mother after she was born!

When you've been in showbusiness as long as I have you get to hear every excuse in the book. (Not *this* book, I just mean metaphorically, of course!) It's one of those professions where one day for posterity you're putting your handprint in cement and the next day you're the one that's mixing it. So as not to appear a failure people make excuses. Having been gifted with a true clear soprano voice from a very early age I've never found any need to make excuses for any shortcomings in our performances; if anything has ever gone wrong it has always been Evadne's fault.

I am delighted that my young friend, Paul James, has put together this collection for it provides me with some perfect excuses for getting my own back after over thirty years! Now I have reasons for not drinking Evadne's herbal tea (it burnt a hole in the hall carpet), getting out of visiting her mother in Scotland, and accounting for that discrepancy in the . . . yes, well that was nothing to do with me anyway, I wasn't even there at the time . . .

HILDA BRACKET D.B.E.
Stackton Tressle

INTRODUCTION

"Two wrongs never make a right, but they make a wonderful excuse."

This book would have been written two years ago, but the dog was pregnant again, we had that dreadful winter, it was simply ages before I could get someone to put the 'S' back on the typewriter, father had croup, and then we had the builders in . . .

Excuses, excuses . . . we all make them, not just to our bosses, our friends, our family, our lovers, but even to ourselves. Smiling wistfully into the mirror we sigh:
'Goodness, I'm getting more laughlines,' and never, 'God! I'm getting old and wrinkled!'
To make excuses for getting fat we cry:
'It's the new metric sizes – they make clothes slightly smaller than they used to.'
Yes, we all make excuses.

An old Malay proverb sums it up by saying that 'anyone unable to dance blames the unevenness of the floor'. Not that we make excuses with the intention of telling a deliberate untruth (well, maybe just the teeniest white lie) but more to ease ourselves out of an otherwise embarrassing position; to pour oil on troubled waters when the situation is potentially explosive, or simply to let someone down gently when the truth is likely to hurt.

When a friend has been pouring out her problems over the telephone for more than an hour and you are bored rigid with the saga of Clive's impotence and Millicent's prolapse, it is much more convincing to say:
'Sorry to rush you, Agatha, but my husband has just come in and has an urgent business call to make.'
or to scream:
'Oh my God! The dog's been in the laundry basket again

and is walking around outside with my knickers in his mouth
– must go!'
than to tell the woman that she is really boring the pants off
you!

Excuses, excuses . . . the situations when we need them are
endless, but don't believe that old adage that 'any excuse is
better than none', it isn't. That misguided gem was simply
put about by someone who couldn't think of a better excuse!
'Credibility' is the key word if your excuse is to be really
convincing, and if only people in history had used their wits
life today might be very different. If only Adam had said:
   'Sorry Lord, but with the sun coming through the branches
it looked just like a pear tree.'
or if Hitler had said:
   'I think I've got a dose of Summer 'flu, let's cancel the trip to
Poland boys.'

Guy Fawkes could have claimed that he thought he was
putting barrels of beer in the Parliament cellars; King Alfred
might have blamed his burnt cakes on the fact that he was
using someone else's oven, and Anne Boleyn would have kept
her head had she one night said:
   'I need some fresh air. I'm just nipping out for a walk round
the block, Hen,' and then fled the country! With just a few
good excuses events could have taken a very different turn.

Making excuses is an art, which comes naturally to some,
others have mastered, and all can learn. The quick-thinking
hostess whose soufflé sinks as flat as a pancake between oven
and table will say:
   'Oh, thank goodness it's worked. This is an old Turkish
recipe. I do love foreign dishes, don't you?' without batting an
eyelid!

The handyman whose shelves collapse before his eyes can
blame the builder who plastered the wall, the incompetence
of the screwmaker, or innocently claim that he was
performing a safety standards test and had deliberately
sabotaged the woodwork.

The problem today, however, when as Browning put it 'the truth sounds bitter', is coming up with a new and original excuse. Nothing is more embarrassing than reaching the end of an elaborate explanation and receiving the cynical response of 'pull the other one, it's got bells on', or 'I haven't just dropped off a Christmas tree, you know!'

Hence, this book. If you've already killed off five grandmothers and the 'afternoon off for a funeral' excuse is wearing a bit thin; if you've genuinely got a headache but your husband's never going to believe it; or you were three feet away from the mouth of the goal and you still didn't score, then simply dip into 'EXCUSES, EXCUSES . . .' and you'll soon discover that no problem is so big that you can't talk your way out of it!

PAUL JAMES

ANY FOOL CAN TELL THE TRUTH
The Art of Making Excuses

"Any fool can tell the truth, but it requires a man of some sense to know how to tell a lie well."
SAMUEL BUTLER

Keeping your wits sharpened is essential if you are going to make excuses successfully, but not so sharp that you end up cutting yourself! A banking friend of mine was out shopping with his wife one day when suddenly this luscious blonde standing on a corner waved to him, giggled and blew a kiss in his direction. Pretending that he hadn't seen her, he turned up his collar against the wind and hurried by. Too late! His eagle-eyed wife demanded to know who the blonde was.

'Oh, just a woman I met last week, professionally, of course,' he explained.

'Oh yes?' said his wife, 'Whose profession? Yours or hers?'

As with all things, there is a right way and a wrong way to make excuses, and there is simply no excuse for coming up with the wrong one! Here are the TEN golden rules to follow:

Rule 1
Only use one excuse at a time.
Many people feel that they are justifying their behaviour by coming out with a whole string of excuses and a complete series of events that led up to their being late, or having failed to meet a deadline. This convinces nobody, and instead of getting them off the hook tends to land them even deeper into the mire. The more excuses you give, the more questionable your story becomes.

'You mean to say, Miss Jones, that after the fire brigade had put out your chip pan fire, and your great-Aunt Ena had been taken to the infirmary, that your bus actually crashed into a tree on the way here? Just not your day, is it Miss Jones?' Your only hope is that your whole story will be dismissed because it is too lengthy and complicated to delve into. Always remember that one excuse is far more convincing.

Rule 2
Remember what you have said and stick to it.
They say that liars need good memories, and if you are going to make up excuses it is essential to remember exactly *what* you have said if you don't want to be found out. The easiest way to slip up is to give two people a different excuse. Friends usually have memories like an elephant and will remember what you've told them years later.

'It was that night you stayed at John's place, don't you remember?'

'Me? Stay at John's place? I've never been there in my life!'

'But, you said . . .'

Whoops! Remember what excuses you have made!

Rule 3
Be confident.
Be sincere, even if you don't mean it! If you haven't got confidence in your own excuse then you cannot expect others

to have. Speak with authority in your voice and whether it's covering up for the fact that you nipped into the pub for a quick drink on the way home from work:

'This damned idiot swerved right in front of me and missed me by inches. I stopped and had a brandy to prevent delayed shock.'

or getting out of a visit to the mother-in-law:

'You know what I'm like in summer, darling, I'd hate to give your mother prickly heat.'

If you speak with conviction you are bound to be believed!

Rule 4
Be brief.

It was Sir Walter Scott who penned those immortal lines:
'Oh what a tangled web we weave, when first we practise to deceive!' and the quickest way to get tangled up is to enter into a lengthy explanation, because if you're trying to go into detail about something that never really happened in the first place, sooner rather than later you are going to become unstuck. Never try and dilute a thirty-second excuse with an hour long explanation!

Rule 5
Never make an excuse when the truth is inevitable.

Human nature entices us to take the easy way out, which is why we still make excuses even though at the back of our mind we know that the truth is bound to be discovered in the end. The consequences are frequently far more painful than if we'd simply told the truth in the first place! Suffering from an almighty hangover, a friend of mine decided to have the day off work. Thinking of what appeared to be an original and conceivable excuse, he put his absence down to the fact he had spent too long on a sunbed on the previous evening and now had painful, peeling skin like a lobster. Marvellous! Until, of course, it dawned on him that on the following day, when he wanted to go back to work, he realised that his skin was lily-white ...

Rule 6
Don't dwell on your excuse.
Doubtless you will feel very relieved when an excuse you make is accepted straightaway without question, but avoid the temptation to keep harking back to it. Don't say half-an-hour later:

'Oh, it was awful, you know. I really haven't got over it yet.'
You may feel that you are adding weight, but you could be creating doubt.

Rule 7
Never say 'You do believe me, don't you?'
This instantly sheds suspicion upon your actions. If you explain a genuine situation that has happened to you, you don't feel a need to ask if you are believed. It doesn't matter whether you were believed because you *know* the truth. Strangely, people making deliberate excuses feel the need to seek reassurance. Resist the temptation, it only raises doubts.

Rule 8
Never use the same excuse twice.
However well an excuse went down, don't try and use it again – at least, not with the same person. It may have been believed once, but despite an oscar-winning performance a second time may be stretching your luck just a little too far!

Rule 9
Keep your excuses credible.
Just because you have got yourself into a big mess doesn't necessarily mean that you need a big excuse to get out of it! It was Adolf Hitler in 'Mein Kampf' who wrote:

'The great masses of the people . . . will more easily fall victims to a big lie than to a small one.'
That was in 1924, but who would believe his excuses now!

Rule 10
Make sure that anyone else involved is in on the story!
It's all very well giving your parents the excuse that you are spending the night at Bob's house after the snooker tourna-

ment, when you will really be tucked up with Lusty-Linda from the local gasboard, but DO remember to tell Bob and Lusty-Linda too! It's amazing how many people neglect this small point, so that when mother telephones Bob's number to remind you to put on clean socks, to tell you that the dog has had another fit, and that grandma's lost her teeth again, you'll find that you need a really good excuse to talk your way out of that one!

Make sure too that if anyone else is involved in any of your excuses that they are going to give exactly the same story as you. A policeman on duty noticed a car being driven rather erratically down the road; it mounted the pavement on two occasions and then proceeded to turn into a road marked 'No Entry' and stopped dead. The policeman went over to the car and asked the driver what he was doing.

'The car went out of control, something to do with the steering,' began the man.

'Oh, don't take any notice of him,' said his wife in the passenger seat, 'He's drunk!'

Should your excuses fail, for any reason, you can relax in the knowledge that you can always blame the Ten Golden Rules!

NOTHING IS IMPOSSIBLE

Executive Excuses

"Nothing is impossible for the man who can find someone else to do it for him."

pp ANON.

The secret of being an executive, as anyone in authority will know, is not to 'do' but to delegate. Ambrose Bierce in his sardonic but disarmingly true 'Devil's Dictionary' insists that if anything is worth doing, it is worth the trouble of asking someone to do it for you. Here are twenty excuses that will enable you to delegate anything.

1 "I know that this is your forte, Mr Hooper, an area in which you excel. Naturally I would have written the report myself, but I thought, what better than to ask the expert."

2 "I have one of those dreadfully boring business lunches at the Ritz. I'd send you along, but I feel that I must attend myself. *Such* a bore."

3 "I shall be in a meeting all afternoon, and this must be done by two o'clock."

4 "It's part of your job."

5 "You're the only one that understands the filing system."

6 "Our department is much too busy, why don't you get the Press Office on to it?"

7 "I think I shall be on a business conference that week, so you'd better handle it."

8 "It will only take you a few minutes. I've got more important things to attend to."

9 "I'm taking this home to finish as I need peace and quiet, you can hold the fort this afternoon."

10 "You start it off, and I'll come and help you just as soon as I have time." (Unfortunately you never do have time!)

11 "You're so much better at dealing with figures than I am."

12 "I think it would sound so much better coming from you. You know exactly how to handle him over the telephone."

13 "You'll have to go. I have to stay and wait for an important telephone call from New York."

14 "You'll get it finished quicker than anyone else, I know that I can rely on you."

15 "This will do so much to help your chances of promotion."

16 "I know that it's an area that you very much enjoy, so I've said you'll do it."

17 "Don't complain. I've got the MacPherson contract to sort out. If we don't get that, you won't have a job at all!"

18 "The computer always goes wrong if I use it."

19 "Head Office specifically recommended that you do it."

20 "I want you to do it, because then I know that it will be a job well done."

Where Industrial Relations are concerned the high-powered executive needs every excuse in the book when acting as the middle-man between the workers and management. To tell the truth could be simply asking for trouble . . .

Excuse "We will consider your claim for higher wages."
The Truth "You're wasting your time."

Excuse "The Managing directors could possibly be persuaded by manipulative methods."
The Truth "You could try bribery."

Excuse "The Supervisor and the Managing Directors are currently involved in negotiations to settle the pay dispute."
The Truth "They are having an argument."

Excuse "The 10% wage increase will come into operation from next June."
The Truth "This will put you into a higher tax bracket, so you'll wish you'd never asked for a rise."

Excuse "The manager is not available to negotiate your claim."
The Truth "He is hiding in the executive toilet."

Excuse "The manager is discussing the proposition with the Union Shop Steward."
The Truth "He has taken him out to lunch to try and make him see reason."

Excuse "Management and staff have come to an agreement."
The Truth "The Management were forced to give in."

Excuse "The workforce are satisfied with the new pay settlement."
The Truth "They promise that it will be at least ten days before they ask for their next wage increase."

Excuse "The men have agreed not to picket the factory."
The Truth "No one wanted to stand around in the cold doing nothing."

One of the perks of a managerial position is the responsibility of hiring and firing staff. Some feel that telling someone that they have got to leave is the hardest thing of all. This need not be the case, not if you have the right excuse:

Excuse "Don't you feel that your high abilities are wasted on this job?"
The Truth "We need someone far more competent than you."

Excuse "Is your wife happy with the hours you work?"
The Truth "Don't you think she would prefer you to have a job with longer hours?"

Excuse "Are you really happy working for the company?"
The Truth "Perhaps you would like to resign before I give you the push."

Excuse "You are an intelligent man, how would you like to advance your career?"
The Truth "You are an incompetent fool, why don't you go and work for somebody else?"

Excuse "I care about my employees – I know you're not content here."
The Truth "I care about my business – we're not content with you."

Excuse "Don't you feel that it was time you climbed the ladder a little?"
The Truth "Sod off, and climb someone else's ladder."

Excuse "Haven't you always dreamed of an early retirement?"
The Truth "Push off, you're too old."

Excuse "I'm afraid the company no longer has the financial strength to secure someone as specialised as yourself."
The Truth "You're being made redundant."

Excuse "I am so sorry that we cannot keep your job available."
The Truth "You're fired."

Excuse "I am certain you would prefer a job with less responsibility."
The Truth "You're fired."

"I am afraid this is the age of new technology."
The Truth "You're being replaced by a computer."

When engaging new staff, remember that they too have to make excuses for their shortcomings and inabilities. To help you read between the lines, the following guide is a must for every boss to study and every applicant to understand.

Job descriptions:

"This job is ideal for anyone who is bored with a 9–5 routine."
– You will work every hour God sends.

"Excellent opportunities for promotion."
– Stay with the job twenty years and you might get promoted.

"An opportunity to gain firsthand experience in Public Relations."
– You will be dealing with all the complaints.

"We require an attractive salesperson."
– We want a woman but aren't allowed to say so.

"Full working uniform will be provided."
– We'll give you an overall.

"Excellent opportunity to earn high commission."
– If you don't sell £50,000 worth of the product each week, you don't get any wages.

"Married man required to take over Personnel Department for large company."
– We don't want any poofs around here.

"An excellent opportunity for you to work abroad."
– Nobody else in the company wants to go to Saudi Arabia for three years.

"Join our experienced entertainments team. Vocals an asset, but not essential."
– We want a stripper.

Job applications:

"I have always been interested in your company's work."
– Ever since I saw what salary you were offering.

"I worked as a secretary for two years."
– I used to make the tea in an office.

"I was fully trained."
– I picked it up as I went along.

"I am looking for part-time employment."
– I don't want my husband to know I'm working.

"I would like to settle down permanently in a job."
– I want to save enough money so that I can leave and have a baby.

"I am used to new technology."
– In my last job I was replaced by a computer.

"I have a personal interest in the company."
– I married the chairman's daughter.

"I have always wanted to be a representative."
– I desperately need a company car.

"Experienced in Girl Friday duties."
– Quite enjoy sexual harrassment.

"I got a degree at Oxford."
– I once did a correspondence course when I lived in Reading.

"I have had a life-long ambition to work in insurance."
– This was the only job available, I had to apply.

"I enjoy responsibility and working on my own."
– I don't like people watching over me, or watching the hours I work.

How to reject applicants without telling the truth:

Excuse "We have decided to appoint from within the company."
The Truth "We were going to anyway, but had to make it look fair by advertising."

Excuse "I am afraid that you are much too highly qualified for the job."
The Truth "We wouldn't employ you if you were the last person on earth."

Excuse "Unfortunately you lack the relevant experience."
The Truth "You know too much, we don't want people telling us what to do."

Excuse "We have given the job to someone with the relevant experience and qualifications."
The Truth "We didn't like the look of you."

Excuse "Unfortunately the post is no longer available."
The Truth "It is, but we're not employing you."

Excuse "Unfortunately we need a little more than a receptionist."
The Truth "You can't even type!"

Excuse "Despite your excellent references, we cannot offer you the job."
The Truth "You must have bribed someone to give you references like that; we don't trust you."

We all know that power tends to corrupt, and according to Lord Acton 'absolute power corrupts absolutely', but most executives will agree with the man who said:

'Power can corrupt, but absolute power is absolutely delightful!'

I'M A GOOD GIRL, I AM

Secretarial Excuses

"No: I don't want no gold and no diamonds. I'm a good girl, I am."
GEORGE BERNARD SHAW (Pygmalion)

Forget the speed of shorthand, the number of words that can be typed by ten fingers in a minute, or the grade achieved on your word processing diploma, the skill that any secretary worth her weight in Typex really needs is how to lie convincingly on behalf of her boss. This takes far more than simply mouthing the familiar words:

   'I'm sorry, he's in a meeting at the moment.'

A lawyer, having told his secretary that he was 'out' to anyone that called, was astonished when a client walked into his office.

   'I knew you weren't really out,' said the client, 'Your secretary was working too hard.'

The worst excuse any secretary can use is:

'Mr Howard is out to lunch with his wife.'

If it's Mrs Howard enquiring after her husband, the Job Centre could soon have yet another unemployed secretary on their hands.

Excuses to the client:

"He/she is in conference until three-thirty."

"He/she is negotiating a big contract and has asked not to be disturbed."

"He/she is out of town all day, can I help you?"

"He/she is being interviewed by local radio and I cannot interrupt the recording."

"He/she left a message for you, but I've mislaid it."

"He/she won't be able to see you until tomorrow."

Excuses on the telephone, followed by "Can I take a message?"

9.30am	"I'm afraid he hasn't arrived yet."
10.00am	"He's going to be just a little late in this morning."
11.00am	"He was in earlier, but is at a meeting now."
12 – 3	"He's at lunch."
3.30pm	"He's having a late lunch."
4.00pm	"He'll be tied up until late. Can you ring back tomorrow?"

Excuses to cover secretarial incompetence:

"My pencil broke at a crucial moment."

"The dictaphone/photocopier/computer/word processor/ switchboard broke down."

"The paper got stuck."

"I dropped a box of paper clips down the back."

"It wasn't in the file."

"It fell down the back of the filing cabinet."

"The telephone hasn't stopped ringing – I didn't have time."

"The duplicator got jammed."

"I broke my glasses and couldn't read the shorthand."

"It was a very bad line, I couldn't hear properly."

"Well, it's not how we *used* to do it!"

MEMO TO SECRETARIES:

Remember, when you are in the wrong, that attack is the best form of defence. Snivelling: "I'm sorry, Mr Jones, it won't happen again," will not get you very far when your clerical error has lost the company thirty-two thousand pounds. Instead snap: "If you would learn to write legibly, I might just be able to copy-type accurately!" and slam the bar on your typewriter across forcibly at the same time. This will make your excuse so much more effective.

Secretarial excuses to office philanderers:

"Get off, it's not my equipment!"

"I must have this finished by half-past four."

"Is that my rugby-playing boyfriend outside the door?"

"This'll look good in your annual assessment. Didn't you know that I have to type a report?"

"Oh, all the secretaries on this floor have got VD or TB. Only go for the ones that cough."

"No, I can't see you tonight. I'm expecting a headache."

"I'm not having lunch. I'm saving up my breaks so that I can have Friday off."

"Don't come any closer. My dictaphone short circuits and you could get a very nasty shock."

"Goodness, don't you look like Ronald Reagan from this angle?"

"Hang on, I'm just on my way to get some more Herpes ointment. Fancy a walk to the chemist?"

"While you're on the floor, could you just see if it's your wage slip that fell down behind the filing cabinet?"

All good things come to an end, and there are times when even the worst secretary feels the need for a new job. If you are about to lose a secretary whose done more damage to your company than government cutbacks, or has been of great service but has done very little actual work, you may require a few excuses when called upon to write a reference . . .

Excuse "Miss Jones is a very competent secretary."
The Truth "Miss Jones is very good at making excuses."

Excuse "She is always willing and able."
The Truth "She is a part-time prostitute."

Excuse "She always works to the limits of her capabilities."
The Truth "She is an incompetent idiot, but she tries hard."

Excuse "Her shorthand leaves a little to be desired."
The Truth "Her shorthand is totally illegible."

Excuse "She pays very strict attention to time."
The Truth "She never misses a coffee break."
Excuse "She takes a great pride in her personal appearance."
The Truth "It must be a big effort to look so slovenly."

Excuse "She is very reliable."
The Truth "You can always trust her to do the wrong thing."

Excuse "The company will not be the same without her."
The Truth "We can't wait to see her go."

Excuse "Her experiences have been vast."
The Truth "She's had every man under twenty-five in the building."

Excuse "She is very knowledgeable in her field."
The Truth "She thinks she knows it all."

SMILE AND BE A VILLAIN

Business Excuses

"O villain, villain, smiling, damned villain!
My tables — meet it is I set it down,
That one may smile, and smile, and be a villain."

HAMLET

The art of being successful in business is knowing which excuse to use and when! Unfortunately, behind any business-man looms a creditor, an unpacified bank manager, or the Inland Revenue. So, remember Rule 3 (Be confident!) and use some of the following:

To the Tax Inspector:

Excuse "I thought I was eligible for tax relief on that?"
The Truth "I had hoped that you wouldn't notice the tax fiddle."

Excuse "My partner balanced the annual accounts."
The Truth "You're not going to blame me for any discrepancies."

Excuse "Owing to the economic climate we only made a very marginal profit."
The Truth "We made a very large profit, but it does not appear on our Tax Return."

Excuse "My overheads are very high."
The Truth "My wife has got very expensive tastes."

To the Accountant:

Excuse "I have considered liquidating personal assets as you suggest, but it just wouldn't be financially viable."
The Truth "I refuse to sell my car and travel by bike as you suggest."

Excuse "I had slight problems with the balance sheet this year."
The Truth "It doesn't balance."

Excuse "We have lots of big contracts under discussion, so the next financial year is looking much brighter."
The Truth "That will keep you happy for this year, and pray to God we get a contract before next April!"

To the Bank Manager:

Excuse "What is collateral security again? I've forgotten."
The Truth "I don't know what the hell you're talking about, but I must appear intelligent."

Excuse "I always pay by cheque, it helps me keep account of my expenditure."
The Truth "I never have enough cash, and being overdrawn just a little bit more can't make any difference."

Excuse "Yes, our account is in the red, but you have to speculate to accumulate, as they say."
The Truth "We're broke."

To Creditors:

"I don't think that the cheque has been cleared yet, but it should be through any day now."
The Truth "I haven't written the cheque yet, but we'll blame the bank for the delay."

Excuse "I would like to query our account."
The Truth "I want to waste a bit more time so that we can afford to pay it."

Excuse "We have put a cheque in the post to you today."
The Truth "We will write one next week and back date it."

Of course, if you are dealing with other companies, or the mere general public, then a whole new set of excuses are at your disposal.

Excuse "We are still waiting for the part to arrive."
The Truth "We haven't got round to ordering the part yet."

Excuse "Unfortunately our company is unable to handle your project at the moment."
The Truth "We never deal with such rubbish."

Excuse "Our men have too much work on at the moment to undertake any more contracts."
The Truth "The men are on strike."

Excuse "We are not in a position to consider your offer at this time."
The Truth "We're bankrupt."

Excuse "Our cash is all tied up at the moment."
The Truth "We are in debt."

Excuse "We have had to call in a specialist."
The Truth "We couldn't do it ourselves."

Excuse "We are extremely busy and will get round to it just as soon as we can."
The Truth "We couldn't really give a damn and we'll do it when we feel like it."

Excuse "We have a staff shortage at the moment."
The Truth "We have just made 300 men redundant."

Excuse "We have a lot of staff on holiday."
The Truth "The men are working to rule."

Excuse "This is the first time that we have tackled such a project on a large scale."
The Truth "We've never done it before and haven't got a clue what we're doing."

Excuse "Unfortunately the firm we deal with sent the wrong component parts."
The Truth "Our engineer is incompetent."

For anyone seeking an investment from you:

Excuse "All our capital is tied up at present."
The Truth "We're still trying to pay off all our debts."

Excuse "The funds are not as high as they used to be."
The Truth "There are no funds available."

Excuse "Perhaps you would like to invest some capital in our company?"
The Truth "We desperately need money!"

Ten Excuses on which to blame the collapse of any business:

1 The Government	2 The Recession
3 The Interest Rate	4 The fall in the Pound
5 The Common Market	6 The 1984/5 Miner's Strike
7 Foreign competition	8 Death of Financial backer
9 Shortage of world resources	10 The Industrial climate

Memo to ensure that you are *never* in the wrong!

"I know you believe you understand what you think I said, but I am not sure you realise that what you heard is not what I meant."

Regrets . . .
". . . It is regretted that we were unable to send the enclosed forms to you before the date by which, had you received them, you would be required to forward completed copies to this office."

To employees:
"If the amount of cash in your paypacket does not agree with the net wages on your payslip, inform the wages clerk in the Treasurer's Office *before* breaking the seal. No errors can be rectified once the seal is broken."

Almost two thousand years ago the Roman satirist, Petronius, gave some invaluable advice which is just as relevant today. "A man who is always ready to believe what is told him will never do well, especially the businessman." Even if you are the one who is always making the excuses, remember when dealing with other businesses that you certainly aren't the only one! He who is the boldest gets away with it.

MISS OTIS REGRETS

Telephone Excuses

"Miss Otis regrets, she's unable to lunch today..."
COLE PORTER

If ever there was a heavensent opportunity for making excuses, Alexander Graham Bell's invention must surely tinkle like the sound of angel's harps! Courtesy of British Telecom the world is your oyster. You can make any excuse you like, for you can't be seen, your blushes go unnoticed, you could be telephoning from anywhere on earth, and if the worst comes to the worst you can always cut off the line. Strange how telephones go dead at the most inopportune moments, isn't it? At least, that's your excuse and you're sticking to it! If you cannot come up with an appropriate excuse then use the telephone by *not* making a call...

"I searched for hours for a telephone, and then when I found one it was out of order, so there was no way I could let you know."

Practically any excuse in the book can be used over the telephone, if said with conviction, but what is missing from your Yellow Pages is a 'get out clause'. Just how do you bring a telephone conversation to a hasty conclusion? Excuses, excuses . . .

1 "Well I could stand here and chat for another hour, but we don't want to run up your 'phone bill any more, do we?" (Chuckle jovially and say goodbye.)

2 "There seems to be something wrong with my dial, it's full of holes . . ." (Cut off the line.)

3 Scream: "Oh my God, here comes Norris!" and put down the receiver. You need never explain who Norris is!

4 "Must go, the dog's just chewing up the cat."

5 "Must dash, the cat's just scratched the dog's eyes out."

6 "Must fly, the cat's just swallowed the budgie."

7 "One of the children has just wandered outside completely naked. (End the conversation before they realise that your youngest is 19.)

8 "I'm waiting for British Telecom to come and mend the 'phone."

9 "We're expecting a call from George's mother and she has an epileptic fit if she can't get through first time."

10 "I haven't given you a blow-by-blow account of our fortnight in Majorca with Doreen and Cecil yet, have I? Oh, must you go?" (Let *them* end the conversation!)

11 "I've got the most dreadful cold, I'd hate to pass any of my germs down the line."

12 "Grandad's got his head stuck down the lavatory trying to retrieve his teeth. The ambulance is on its way, but I must keep the line clear."

13 Whisper: "I just heard breaking glass and now someone is walking around upstairs. I think I'd better go and investigate."

14 "My eldest is cooking dinner, and I'm not sure I can trust her with the electric carving knife."

15 "We were *just* going out of the door. I'd love to stop and talk, but we'd hate to keep the President/Queen/Managing Director/Pope/Ambassador/Viceroy/Earl/Duke/Captain waiting."

16 "I'm afraid we're in the middle of a crisis. I'll ring you back." (Slam down the receiver; don't ring back.)

17 "My ex-wife/husband has just walked past the window. I must pretend I'm out."

18 Suddenly begin saying: "Hello? . . . Hello? . . . Hello-o?" each in a different tone and then put down the receiver. If the person rings back, keep saying "Hello?" until they get bored.

19 "We're expecting a call from Australia/America/Bangkok/Gabon/Mauritania; they always ring about this time."

20 "Smoke seems to be coming out of the receiver, I think I'd better go before I get electrocuted."

As a final resort, and if nothing else will work, simply scream:
    "Oh my God!" and slam down the receiver.

The very first words ever spoken on a telephone were to a Mr Thomas A. Watson on March 10th, 1876, when Alexander Graham Bell uttered the immortal words: "Mr Watson, come here; I want you." Whatever happened after that was their own affair, but more than a century later we seem to spend more time trying to politely say: "I don't want you!" but naturally we never say quite what we mean . . .

Excuse "I'm afraid she's in the bath at the moment."
The Truth "She doesn't want to talk to you."

Excuse "I'm sorry, Richard, she's out with her new boyfriend Tony."
The Truth "She's on the bed crying her eyes out."

Excuse "What a surprise to hear from you."
The Truth "How the hell did you discover my new number?"

Excuse "Yes, do give me a call. The number is in the book."
The Truth "We're ex-directory, you'll never find us."

Excuse "I must go, there's someone at the door."
The Truth "I can't waste time talking to you."

Excuse "I'm sure he'll call you back just as soon as he can."
The Truth "You'll never hear from him again."

Excuse "How unfortunate, I think we got cut off."
The Truth "My hand accidentally on purpose touched the receiver rest."

The worst occasion of all is when you *know* that someone is going to telephone and under no circumstance do you want to talk to them. It's all very well to get someone to explain that you're out, but sooner or later the question is going to be asked: 'Where were you?' or 'Why didn't you leave a message, you knew I was going to ring?' In this instance, whoever answers the telephone on your behalf needs a slightly more original excuse.

1 "She's stuck in a new Yoga position and can't move out of the bedroom."

2 "He's had another attack of pleurisy, but he should be up and about in a month or so."

3 "She's cracked a bone in her foot and can't walk to the 'phone."

4 "He's gone away for a short break. Try ringing again in about six months time."

5 "She's got one of her 'throats', but we're hoping she'll get her voice back in a few days."

6 "He's out canvassing for the local by-elections."

7 "She's just joined the squash/tennis/swimming/rugby/
football/ten-pin bowling/windsurfing club. We never see
her these days, she spends every spare minute there."

8 "The dog's having puppies and he's acting as midwife. I
couldn't possibly disturb him now."

9 "She took two sleeping pills by mistake. They look just
like aspirins. Now it's like trying to raise the dead."

10 "He wants to finish reading *War and Peace* before his
class tomorrow and I'm not to disturb him. He's already
on Chapter Five, so I don't suppose he's got much further
to go."

CALL BACK YESTERDAY

Excuses for being Late

"O! call back yesterday, bid time return."
SHAKESPEARE

There's only one thing worse than being late and that is having to explain the reason why! Frequently we have no control over our delay. The telephone rings just as you are leaving the house; the traffic lights are against you; the bus is full and goes by without stopping; the train stops yards short of the station for no explicable reason; all perfectly genuine excuses, yet when you bluster into the office twenty minutes late they somehow sound inadequate. Far worse than being late for work, of course, is arriving home late. That always requires an excuse that will stand up to interrogation. My young niece once asked her mother why fairy stories always began 'Once upon a time...'

'They don't always, dear,' said her mother. 'The ones your father tells usually start, "Sorry I'm late dear, I got held up at the office."'

In 1742 Edward Young penned the words 'Procrastination is the thief of time', but I prefer dear old Oscar Wilde's parody: *Punctuality* is the thief of time'! If punctuality is never your strong point, use an excuse . . .

Sorry I'm late home dear, but:

1 "There was a strike by ticket collectors and they wouldn't let us off the platform."

2 "My trousers went at the seam and I had to wait at one of those invisible menders before I could come home."

3 "My crown came loose, but I managed to get an emergency appointment at the dentist at 6.30, wasn't that lucky?"

4 "I had to wait for a call from Hong Kong, you know what the time difference is like."

5 "I felt ill this afternoon and had to go to sick bay. God knows what the sister gave me, but I didn't come round until gone seven."

6 "It's your birthday next month and I had to go and order your present in advance."

7 "The tail of my coat got caught in the bus door; I had to run all the way to Watford before I could get free."

8 "That woman you hate across the road was just coming in the gate as I arrived home. I knew you wouldn't want to see her, but it took me twenty minutes to get rid of her."

9 "You mean you didn't have the blizzard here?"

10 "The boss had one of his heart murmurs. I volunteered to run him to the hospital. Well, it could mean promotion, sweetheart."

To be late home from work, you need to have arrived at work in the first place. Arriving is one thing, arriving *on time* is another.

I would have been here on time, but:

1 "A tree fell down and not only blocked my garage, but pulled down the telephone wires so that I couldn't even ring you."

2 "We've got a new clock-radio and I must have set it to come on in the evening instead of the morning."

3 "The dog chewed through the wires on my radio-alarm."

4 "I usually have an alarm call, but the operator overslept."

5 "My son put water in my petrol tank, you know what kids are like."

6 "We had an intruder in the night. Nothing stolen, but I had to have the police in to check for fingerprints."

7 "My husband/wife/child was ill in the night. I nearly wasn't able to come in at all today, but I decided that my work must come before my family."

8 "There was a bomb scare and all the streets around my home were cordoned off. There was simply nothing I could do."

9 "The nextdoor neighbour's house burned down in the night. Anyone got a home for two orphans?"

10 "You mean it's *next* week that we put the clocks back?"

Far worse than being late for work is being late for a rendez-vous with a friend or partner. A French proverb says that men count up the faults of those that keep them waiting, and having one friend who is never on time I can certainly vouch for that. On one memorable occasion I literally dragged myself from my sick bed to meet in a bar at 7.00pm. At 7.45pm the barman called me to the telephone. It was my friend.

'Sorry, I've been held up,' came a chirpy voice, 'actually I'm working for the Samaritans and I've got a suicidal case here,

but I should be back with you in half-an-hour.'
I went back to my corner and immersed myself in a double gin. Eight o'clock. Eight-thirty. Nine o'clock. Nine-thirty. It was just approaching ten o'clock and I was feeling like death warmed up, when in he breezed. No word of apology. Instead he slapped me on the back and cried:

'Oh it is lovely to see you again, and you're looking *so* well!' It was only the thought of a prison cell that prevented homicide with malice. If anyone keeps me waiting now they have to have a very very good excuse!

I'm sorry to keep you waiting, but:

1. "I came out of the sauna this afternoon and someone had gone off with all my clothes. What could I do?"

2. "You might have said *which* King's Arms, I've been round half a dozen trying to find you."

3. "Surely you said nine o'clock, not half-past eight? I even wrote it down."

4. "I wanted to bring this bottle of wine, but I had to wait because the off-licence was closed. It's run by such a dizzy queen, she never opens on time."

5. "Why are you waiting outside Harrods? You distinctly said Harvey Nichols – I've been there over an hour."

6. "I wanted to buy you a little present, but there was such a queue; I waited there for over twenty minutes and then I gave up."

7. "*You* were late, I came here a bit early and when you didn't arrive I went off for a walk."

8. "I didn't think you'd be on time. You never are, so I didn't bother to hurry."

9. "I got stuck in a lift in that multi-storey car park. I left myself plenty of time, and then that had to go and happen."

10. "Didn't you get my message that I was going to be late?"

To be late once is forgivable; to keep the same person waiting on more than one occasion is a crime. Sadly, experience teaches that some people are always behind time, however hard they try. 'Punctuality,' said Louis XVIII, 'is the politeness of kings', and throughout King George V's reign the clocks at Sandringham were deliberately kept half-an-hour fast. This ensured that most people were in the right place at the right time, except the young Lady Elizabeth Bowes-Lyon who was persistently late for dinner. Melting all hearts even then, King George would excuse her, saying:

'You are not late, my dear, we must have sat down two minutes early.'

NOT NOW DARLING

Bedroom Excuses

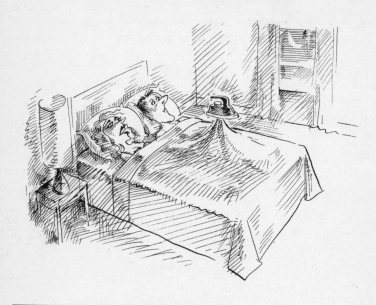

"Not Now Darling."

(Title of a long-running comedy by Ray Cooney)

A recent sex survey revealed that 87% of married women have to initiate love-making at least some of the time, which instantly explodes the myth that men are far more interested in sex. Could this prove the existence of the male menopause?

'Not tonight, Shirley, it's the wrong time of the month.'
Are men really more susceptible to headaches? Something Kinsey never reported! Or is the much quoted 3.5 times a week national average a mere lie put about by those that compile sex surveys? The only time some couples are compatible is when they *both* have a headache!

If you feel more like curling up with a cup of cocoa and a good book than sinking into your partner's arms, turn the other cheek and say . . .

I'd love to, darling, but:

1 "You know I've got to be up early in the morning."

2 "It'll be much better on Saturday."

3 "I think the children are still awake. You know how the bed springs creak."

4 "That pain's come right across the middle of my back again."

5 "Lie still, I've just ironed these sheets."

6 "I had garlic for lunch."

7 "I've just taken two sleeping pills. If only you'd said a few minutes earlier."

8 "I must just go down for another pickled onion first."

9 "I want to finish this chapter. Go to sleep and I'll wake you up when I'm ready."

10 "You know I haven't got my American Express card."

Although a refusal often offends, it is far better than starting something that you cannot finish. Distracting your partner's attention by saying 'that ceiling's got a nasty crack in it.' or 'isn't that a damp patch over there?' won't help much either. To explain your sexual inadequacies you need to explain just why the earth didn't move . . .

Sorry about that, darling, but:

1 "I think I must have ruptured myself carrying your shopping home from the supermarket."

2 "I keep getting a shock from these nylon sheets."

3 "For a minute you looked just like my last husband."

4 "I can't concentrate if you keep snoring."

5 "I should never have had that last gin and orange."

6 "I can never perform when there's an 'R' in the month."

7 "Perhaps we were trying too hard."

8 "I can't help thinking that the vasectomy might not have worked."

9 "You know what they say, you can't be successful every time."

10 "If only you'd worn that mask over your face like I told you."

Excuses need not be negative, of course, and there are times (3.5 a week?) when you want to do something more in bed than just sleep. If your bedmate is lying like the iceberg that sank the 'Titanic', and any mention of the missionary position might result in your head being bitten off, you need a much more subtle excuse ...

Come on, darling:

1 "It'll cure your headache."

2 "It'll put some colour back in your cheeks."

3 "You won't need to finish knitting those bedsocks."

4 "It'll help get rid of that excess fat around your thighs."

5 "This'll be better than a hot water bottle."

6 "Don't you really want to know what it's like being in bed with Richard Gere/Joan Collins?"

7 "Your winceyette nightwear just arouses uncontrollable desires in me."

8 "It's October the third again."

9 "You couldn't just massage the small of my back could you, I think I might have pulled a muscle?"

10 "The batteries on my vibrator have run out, I just don't know what to do."

If your partner merely turns over with a grunt, and the lump beside you looks more like a killer whale than John Travolta, your only consolation is to think back to the Roman play-wright Seneca's advice, when he wrote in a letter:

'No one can have all he wants, but a man can refrain from wanting what he has not, and cheerfully make the best of a bird in the hand.'

I wonder if it loses something in the translation?

TO HELL, MY LOVE!

Excuses for Unwanted Admirers

> *"Now I know the things I know,*
> *And do the things I do;*
> *And if you do not like me so,*
> *To hell, my love, with you!"*
> DOROTHY PARKER

She chewed furiously on her gum. Took a long draw on her cigarette and exhaled a cloud of nicotine fumes in the face of the lecherous creep that was trying to chat her up.

'Haven't I seen you on the telly?' she drawled.

'You might have,' said the man, preening himself.

'Yeh, I have. It's called *interference!*'

If you have the courage, a put-down is the simplest way to deflate an unwanted admirer, but the more persistent hangers-on need more than their ego dented to get the message across. The super smooth guys with a slick line in chat-up patter will soon be put off if you say:

1 "I can only talk to you for a minute, my boyfriend will be back from his karate class any second."

2 "Can't stop, I'm just off to the ante-natal clinic."

3 "Well, nearly time for my judo lesson . . ."

4 "I thought for a minute that you were my boyfriend's grandfather. The resemblance in uncanny."

5 "You don't happen to know where the lesbian-feminist group is meeting do you?"

6 "Don't stand too close, I'd hate you to catch anything."

7 "Sorry, I don't drink. Not since the hepatitis."

8 "My boyfriend loves to take things apart to see why they won't go. Perhaps you'd better go."

9 "Oh, isn't your wife looking pretty today. That is her over there isn't it?"

10 "I'd love to have dinner on Wednesday, and I know my date will. Have you got someone that can make up a foursome?"

'A compliment,' wrote Victor Hugo, 'is like a kiss through a veil.' Napoleon went even further and claimed that anyone who knows how to flatter also knows how to slander. So, you can be certain that if anyone pays you a compliment there is usually an ulterior motive, or perhaps it is just an excuse to avoid saying what is really meant. They may also present yet one more opportunity to chat you up . . .

Excuse "You really do have very distinctive eyes."
The Truth They are a lovely shade of red."

Excuse "You have a very beautiful body."
The Truth "I want to get it into bed."

Excuse "I've never met anyone like you before."
The Truth "Is there another one as peculiar as you?"

Excuse "I admire brains in a woman."
The Truth "I'd rather have your body than your brain."

Excuse "I couldn't help noticing the unusual straps on your shoes."
The Truth "I'm into leather and bondage."

Excuse "I much prefer the more mature woman."
The Truth "All the young girls here have turned me down, there's only you left."

Excuse "As soon as I saw you across the room, I simply knew that you were something special."
The Truth "I couldn't help noticing your gold American Express card."

Should the worst occur and you find yourself alone, unchaperoned and positively too close for comfort with your unwanted admirer, to keep your reputation, virginity and lip-gloss intact, there's only one thing to do. Keep your legs crossed, your arms folded and your tongue sharpened ...

Boy: "We could make wonderful music together."
Girl: "Sorry. I'm tone deaf."

Boy: "Wouldn't you be more comfortable on the settee?"
Girl: "No, I feel quite at home behind the piano."

Boy: "It's very cold in bed alone."
Girl: "Remind me to buy you a hot water bottle."

Boy: "You can stay the night if you want."
Girl: "Why, is the spare bed made up?"

Boy: "All the other girls do."
Girl: "Must be very refreshing for you to find a girl that doesn't."

Boy: "Can I sit beside you?"
Girl: "Can't you see me from where you're sitting?"

Boy: "I've never been with a girl before."
Girl: "Well, when you do, write and tell me what it was like."

Boy: "What a pity, you've missed your last bus."
Girl: "What a blessing my father's a taxi driver."

Boy: "Have another drink?"
Girl: "Yes, a hot chocolate before I go would be lovely, thank you."

Boy: "Did I ever show you my bedroom?"
Girl: "No, I must come and have a look at it in daylight sometime."

Boy: "You'll never know what you've missed."
Girl: "You don't miss what you don't know."

No one is infallible and sadly you cannot have people on ten day's trial and return them undamaged if they prove to be unsuitable. Unfortunately when God gave us emotions, He forgot to include an instruction leaflet as a guide to turning them on and off. This means that when your date is switched on and the bells are ringing, and you are decidedly switched off, what do you do? One of the most difficult aspects of any relationship is ending it. Crippen buried his under the cellar floor; Henry VIII resorted to execution, and Lucrezia Borgia could certainly tell us a thing or two about putting out old flames. Forget the violence, let someone down gently . . .

I'd love to spend the rest of my life having a deeply meaningful relationship with you, but:

1 "You deserve somebody much better."

2 "I've got a job abroad for two years."

3 "I just couldn't live with your mother."

4 "I could never make you happy."

5 "It would be much nicer to be just friends."

6 "You could never live with my four dogs, eighteen cats, twenty-two goldfish and baby alligator."

7 "I'm just not cut-out to be a mortician's wife."

8 "I couldn't inflict my disgusting bedroom habits on you."

9 "I'm dead keen on necrophilia, bestiality, and sadism. Maybe I'm flogging a dead horse . . ."

10 "Let's spend some time apart and see if we still feel the same in 1992."

WARNING: Remember when breaking off a relationship that Hell hath no fury like a woman scorned, and Heaven has no rage like love to hatred turned! Nothing is sweeter than revenge, as one airline pilot found to his cost. Having ended his relationship with an air stewardess, he ordered her out of his flat. As he was flying to Australia he gave her time to find herself somewhere else, on the condition that she was gone by the time he returned. True to her word, the flat was empty when he got back, but the telephone was off the hook. As a parting gesture the girl had dialled the speaking clock in New York! 'At the third stroke, your telephone bill will be ...'

LOVE IS LIKE THE MEASLES

Relationship Excuses

"Love is like the measles; we all have to go through it."
JEROME K. JEROME

"Love's like the measles – all the worse when it comes late in life."
DOUGLAS JERROLD

A woman on a tube train thought she recognised her husband in the crush, so she pushed her way towards him and gave him a big hug and a kiss. It turned out to be a complete stranger, totally unknown to her. In an attempt to excuse her actions she said,

'I really am terribly sorry, but your head looks just like my husband's behind.'

Whoops! Not quite what she should have said perhaps, but the approach was certainly right. A case of mistaken identity is an excellent excuse for introducing yourself to any complete stranger that takes your fancy. It gets over the hurdle of making the first move. Your phrasing, however, is all important. Don't for example, say: 'For a minute I thought you were my grandfather.' Your 'mistake' must be flattering! On a bus recently a friend of mine, a primary school teacher, sat opposite a man whom she genuinely felt was familiar to her. Smiling pleasantly, she turned to speak to him, then noticing his lack of response, she realised her error.

'Oh, excuse me,' she said, 'I mistook you for the father of two of my children.'

When an attractive stranger suddenly moves into the house opposite yours and you need an excuse to introduce yourself, there are a number of subtle ways in which you can make your presence felt:

1 Say that you have accidentally dropped a valuable ring down the drain and would he come and help you fish it out.

2 Fall off your bicycle in full view of his/her window. You will need to be taken inside for something strong and sweet to help you recover from the shock.

3 Claim that your telephone is out of order and can you borrow theirs. Pop back later because you forgot to leave money for the call.

4 The next time a fuse blows pretend to be distressed and ask for help.

5 Claim that there is a very worrying tapping noise that appears to be coming from somewhere inside your bedroom. Naturally you are too nervous to investigate alone.

6 Call and see if an 'important letter' that has gone astray has been left at their house in error.

7 Send a letter/parcel to yourself with their number on instead of yours so that it is delivered to them. They will have to call and see you!

8 Find out their telephone number and ring, pretending that you have got the wrong number. Engage them in conversation. What a coincidence that you live within yards of each other . . .

9 Take across a bottle and a corkscrew and say that you cannot get the cork out. For their kindness, invite them across to your party – even if your other guests don't turn up!

10 Keep track of their movements so that you can catch the same bus/train every day. If they have a car, plead a lift one day. If necessary take up cycling.

The art of courtship has been described as a witty prologue to a very dull play. To say what you really mean can be embarrassing, so again it is essential to know what to say, and more importantly exactly what the twinkle in your partner's eyes implies. Is it love or just wind?

Excuse "I'm unattached."
The Truth "I'm desperate for a man."

Excuse "I would climb mountains for you, cross rivers . . ."
The Truth "No, I'm not coming over tonight – not in the rain."

Excuse "Do you think that you and I are totally compatible?"
The Truth "Will you sleep with me?"

Excuse "You and I have far more going for us than just a physical relationship."
The Truth "Your father is worth a fortune and is liable to peg out at any time."

Excuse "My girl friend is different from all the other girls I've known."
The Truth "She's willing to leap into bed any time I want."

Excuse "I want you to have dinner with me."
The Truth "I want to get you drunk and seduce you."

Excuse "Can I drive you home?"
The Truth "Will you let me come home with you."

Excuse "Yes, the man I marry must be virile, strong, good looking . . ."
The Truth "Yes, any man will do."

Excuse "I will not marry him just because he's got money."
The Truth "I wouldn't marry him if he hadn't got money."

Excuse "Do you love me?"
The Truth "Do you like me enough to go to bed with me?"

The relationship that requires the most excuses is the extra-marital one. Not only do you need all the late-home-from-work excuses, but when you are out with your affair and you meet a friend, then you really need help . . .

SHE'S MY:

1 New secretary
2 Accountant
3 Sister
4 Neighbour in distress

5 Sister-in-law
6 Wife's friend
7 Agent
8 Private detective, shh!

9 Niece
10 Researcher

HE'S MY:

1 Personal Assistant
2 Lawyer
3 Brother
4 Neighbour giving me a lift home

5 Brother-in-law
6 Husband's colleague
7 Agent
8 Private detective, not a word!

9 Nephew
10 Elder brother from Australia

I LOVE IT, I LOVE IT

Idle Excuses

"I love it, I love it; and who shall dare
To chide me for loving that old arm-chair?"
ELIZA COOK

Feel like spending the day in bed? Does opening an eye require more effort than running the London Marathon? Having settled yourself in front of the television, does a little nagging voice say: 'The lawn wants cutting, after you've weeded the rosebed, planted those marrows and washed the car . . .'? Yes, there are times when just the very act of living seems a chore, but you know the answer!

Sorry I can't come into work today, but:

1 "It's my back. I can hardly stand up straight." As more

working days are lost through back pain than anything else, you can't go wrong with this one!

2 "It's my wife/husband. Taken ill in the night, I can't possibly leave them until the doctor's been."

3 "What I've got isn't too serious for me, but if a man catches it it can make him sterile. I can come in if you like, Mr Jones?"

4 "I've got an upset stomach and feel dreadfully bilious." Nobody can prove that you haven't!

5 "I think I'm starting a cold, so am going to spend the day in the warm."

6 "I've got some pills from the doctor that make me drowsy; I mustn't drive or use machinery."

7 "I've developed one of my migraine attacks. One of the worst I've ever had."

8 "We had a pipe burst in the night. I can't tell you what the damage is like." Have the tap running while you make the telephone call. If possible, get someone to go 'Glug! Glug!' in the background.

9 "I'm having problems with my wisdom teeth."

10 "The central heating has blown up and I'm waiting for the repair man to come." Repair men can be days late!

An excuse in this instance is always much more convincing if you can get someone to telephone on your behalf, but do synchronise times.

"What does this mean, Miss Peabody? Someone has just telephoned to say that you won't be in today because you're sick."

"That'll be my friend, Marlene. She was supposed to ring tomorrow."

Time off work, even if genuinely taken, rarely means time for relaxation. There are always little jobs to do around the house, from insulating the attic to building a granny flat for your mother-in-law. The most prudent husband will buy his wife the very finest bone china, this will ensure that he will never be trusted with the washing-up! Other household chores need an excuse . . .

1 "I haven't got the right tool for it."

2 "I can't let the neighbours see me working on a Sunday."

3 "The man next door borrowed my ladder."

4 "That needs a professional plumber/builder/carpenter/ electrician; I couldn't risk doing it myself."

5 "I can't, it's raining."

6 "That's a job for the winter, flies will stick to the paint."

7 "I've got too much paperwork to do."

8 "It'll take too long to do today."

9 "I haven't got the right part yet."

10 "I thought you said you'd do it?"

If you are forced into a situation where you have to get out of your chair and work, then do the task at a leisurely pace. With any luck you'll hear:
'Come on, let *me* do it! Otherwise we'll be here 'til doomsday.' Then you can return to your chair. Should anyone criticise you for working slowly, appear very intellectual by quoting Henry Thoreau, who in his journal on 31st March, 1841, wrote:
'The really efficient labourer will be found not to crowd his day with work, but will saunter to his task surrounded by a wide halo of ease and leisure.'
Having knocked them flat with that, it could be some time before you're asked to undertake anything more. At the very least you will be left to continue unhampered.

If you are genuinely idle, the kind of person that needs helping to the floor when you faint; the sort that would only marry someone with children, and nobody knows your true height because you've never been seen standing up, then there must be occasions when you would be quite happy to spend the entire day in bed. For the true lay-about, *any* excuse will do!

I'm not getting up today because:

"It's raining."
"It's Monday."
"I've got a bone in my leg."
"I didn't sleep a wink last night."
"I've got nothing to wear."
"I'm not at all well."
"It's only midday."
"Mother's coming."
"I'm suffering from jet lag."
"I've got a long day ahead of me."
"I need to conserve my energy."
"Nobody will even notice."
"I'd only have to go to bed again tonight anyway."

BETTER THAN A RUDE GRANT

Unacceptable Invitation Excuses

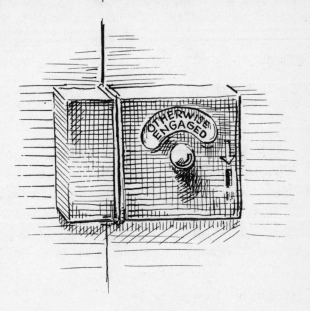

"A civil denial is better than a rude grant."
THOMAS FULLER

It was either Sam Goldwyn or James McNeil Whistler, and probably both, who shook the hand of their hostess at the end of a party and said: 'I've had a wonderful evening. But this wasn't it.' Accepting an invitation to do something that you really will not enjoy is usually far worse than refusing it. Insulting your host is one way of ensuring that you will never be invited back, but unless you happen to be a member of the Royal Family, or in a position to engage your own Private Secretary, refusing invitations invariably requires a very diplomatic excuse.

Whether it is the Brown's tedious drinks party, the local

Woodcarvers' Association annual dinner, great-aunt Edna's forty-ninth wedding anniversary celebrations, or a request to make a speech at an Old Boy's Reunion, an 'otherwise engaged' excuse is frequently the best, preferably a 'long-standing arrangement' that is simply impossible to break. Never decline an invitation by announcing that you have somewhere more important to go, or a function that you would *prefer* to attend; that's not an excuse but an insult!

With a full diary of engagements, Her Majesty the Queen has the advantage of being able to plan her excuses months in advance.

1 "We shall be at Balmoral that weekend."

2 "Charles is playing polo, one must go and watch."

3 "Unfortunately I'm opening parliament that Tuesday."

4 "Sadly I've got the Prime Minister coming."

5 "We'd love to come, but it clashes with one of those boring State Banquets, you know how it is."

6 "I'll be rehearsing my Christmas broadcast."

7 "It's Princess Anne's birthday."

8 "We've got the decorators in at Windsor Castle, otherwise we could have made it."

9 "No, we'll be at Sandringham for the *whole* of January."

10 "That's Ascot week. We couldn't possibly miss that; Philip loves a little flutter."

11 "But you know I'm Trooping the Colour that day!"

12 "No, sorry, it's the Order of the Garter Ceremony that Monday."

13 "We're contemplating another Jubilee that year, drop me a line the year after."

14 "That's right in the middle of my Commonwealth tour, sorry."

15 "It's my turn to suffer the Royal Variety Show this year."

Few of us are fortunate enough to be able to plan ahead with our excuses, but there's nothing to stop us taking a leaf out of Her Majesty's book of Royal Wheezes to suit our own situation . . .

My husband and I would love to accept your invitation, but:

1 "We've arranged a 'Have-it-away' weekend in Bognor."

2 "It's the children's sports day, they'll be so disappointed if we don't go."

3 "We've got George's boss coming to dinner, there's no way we can cancel."

4 "I'm rehearsing with the local Operatic Society that night; yes, I'm 'Mad Margaret' again!"

5 "It's mother's birthday, the one time when the *whole* family gather together."

6 "We're planning a world cruise, so any date in the Summer will be out for us I'm afraid."

7 "*Not* the twenty-fifth! *Any* other date would have been perfect. Oh, *what* a pity."

8 "My brother and sister-in-law are coming over from the States. We couldn't possibly inflict the whole family on you."

9 "The whole house is being re-wired that week. I wouldn't trust the workmen here on their own."

10 "There's a concert that evening. I'd cancel, but we booked the tickets over six months ago, they are *so* difficult to come by."

Planning excuses in advance is all very well, but what happens when you are put on the spot by a sudden telephone call with an invitation you cannot refuse? Be bold and refuse it! Keep the following list beside the telephone:

I'd love to, but:

> "The dog's had a hysterectomy – just off to collect her."
>
> "I've just cooked a huge meal for us."
>
> "I've just taken two sleeping pills – haven't been sleeping too well."
>
> "We're expecting guests of our own at any moment."
>
> "I've got to be up early tomorrow."
>
> "The gas cooker just blew up, any idea how to get curry off the ceiling?"
>
> "I'm babysitting for the neighbours."
>
> "I can't, it's Ramadhan."
>
> "It clashes with prison visiting hours."

An eighteenth century song sums up the true art of refusing invites:

> ... Whom she refuses, she treats still
> With so much sweet behaviour,
> That her refusal, through her skill,
> Looks almost like a favour!

FIND THE TIME IN MY FACE

Excuses for Unwelcome Guests

"My evening visitors, if they cannot see the clock should find the time in my face."

EMERSON

What a sober man has in his heart, a drunken man has on his lips. An ageing actress, who was more than a little worse for drink, was giving a cocktail party that she wished would come to an end. Looking up she saw three late arrivals approaching her, still wearing their coats and thinking that they were guests on the verge of leaving she staggered up to them. Unfortunately her words got mixed around and instead of greeting them as she intended, she cried: 'Oh, must you really stay? Can't you go?'

A slip of the tongue can be one method of encouraging guests that have outstayed their welcome to leave. The artist, Whistler, did not need excuses, he declined to make guests feel welcome in the first place! When a young man jovially said to the artist:

'I passed your house yesterday.'
Whistler replied that he was deeply grateful!

Hospitality is all very well, but there are always some people who linger too long, however subtle your hints. It's 3 a.m. You've been wearing pyjamas for the last two hours, have offered them three cups of Horlicks, thrown a cover over the parrot, laid the table for breakfast, and put out most of the lights, yet still they remain. If you've got guests who simply never get the message, then forget subtlety and begin your excuses from the moment they arrive . . .

On arrival:

"Would you like a small sherry?"
Lock anything stronger away, and give them only small glasses, which you can refill once or twice giving the appearance of generosity. If they've brought a bottle of wine with them, open it immediately and use it as an excuse not to serve anything else.

"Oh, you've parked the car in the road. It will be alright there for at least two hours."
This puts a suggestion in their mind that they have a two-hour limit. Park your car so that it blocks the gate, and forces them into the road.

"Do come and sit down for a minute."
Say this in a jovial and friendly manner, but already you have precluded any idea of a long stay.

"Just put your coats on a chair, we don't stand on ceremony here!"
Coats are then at the ready for a quick exit. Never put the coats of this type of guest in the bedroom, they could stay all night.

"Dinner's ready now, shall we eat straight away?"
If they are the type of long-staying guest that invites

themself to dinner, make sure that it is ready the instant they arrive. You can eat first, then have an hour's chat, before suggesting departure.

After dinner:

"Well, it has been nice to see you again. Pity we've got to be up early in the morning, otherwise we were going to suggest that we went to the theatre first and then ate afterwards." You are still sweetness itself, and have given yet one more display of your generous nature, at the same time making it quite clear that you have to be up early.

"Yes, it is quite chilly. The central heating always goes off at this time."
Having pre-set the heating to go off early, despite the warmth of your smiles, the chill of the room will encourage them to make a move. Even if you have a fireplace, never have a roaring log fire with these guests, the flames attract them like moths.

When you feel that you've had enough:

"Well hasn't this been a pleasant evening. Did you need a lift to the station? We don't want to see you go, but would hate you to miss your train."

This has clearly brought the evening to a close. If they *do* need a lift to the station, then it is yet one more sociable gesture on your part. If they remind you that they came by car, giggle and say how silly of you to forget. Ask what type of car they have. This instantly puts the idea of 'car' into their mind. They might even take you out to have a look at it. If they still remain seated, say:

"I hope your car's alright out there. We've had a lot of vandalism lately."

Now they will move. Any suggestion of damage to people's property instantly gets them going. No guest is going to go outside and check the car and come back in again, so you're almost there.

"Can I help you with your coat?"

If your guest stands up at any point, leap in and say this. What a marvellous host you are! Nothing is too much trouble.

"Do let me see you to the door."
Final friendly gesture. Do this slowly and calmly and your guests will not even realise that they've been ushered out. Say goodbye, smile and wave until they are out of sight. This ensures that they have left.

For the *very* stubborn guest who drops in uninvited and refuses to leave, forget the friendly approach:

1 "Well, we must do the washing-up. Are you going to help *before you go*?"

2 "Time to take the dog out. Shall I walk you to the bus stop, we usually go that way?"

3 "It's great seeing you. Do drop in again sometime." (Give a frosty stare.)

4 "Did we show you the video of our Sybil's wedding?" (This will make them go of their own accord.)

5 "Must throw you out now. The burglar alarm's on a timer and you'll be trapped if you don't go now."

CALL ME EARLY, MOTHER DEAR

Excuses to Leave Early

> *"You must wake and call me early, call me early, mother dear,"*
> TENNYSON

Parties are like sex. There are occasions which are infinitely memorable, but there are times when you wish you'd never made the effort. As with many things in life, the anticipation is often far better than the actual event. It is wise never to go to a party of any kind, however promising it may seem, without a good excuse to get away early up your sleeve. Should the function prove more boring than drilling for North Sea oil, then you have an instant reason to leave. On the other hand, if you discover that you're having a better time than a dog in a lamppost factory then you can easily forget your excuse.

One of the most convincing methods is to get someone to telephone you at the party within the first hour. If you can see that you are going to have fun, then you can tell the person on the other end of the line what a marvellous party it is, but if you feel totally out of place then the call is your excuse to depart.

'But, mother, that's awful! I'll come straight away ...'

Sorry, folks, I've got to leave:

1 "Mother's got caught in her knitting machine and is slowly being unravelled."

2 "A telegram has arrived for me at home. It might be something urgent."

3 "My girlfriend's locked herself out of her flat, I must go and rescue her."

4 "The dog won't take his distemper pill, I'm the only one he trusts. He's already bitten mother, three neighbours and a Jehovah's Witness."

5 "I forgot that I was supposed to be making a speech tonight. That was Alcoholics Anonymous just now."

6 "Someone stole my wallet/handbag this afternoon, that was the police station. I've got to go and identify the man now."

7 "Apparently there's someone at home who's come from abroad to see me. I'd better find out who it is."

8 "That was the hospital. I must dash before I infect you all."

9 "That was the TV studio. They want me in the audience for 'The Price is Right'!"

10 "That was the library. They're really clamping down on overdue books these days. I've got to return them immediately."

If there's nobody that you can bribe to telephone you, then you must go armed with a ready-made excuse:

I can't stop long:

1 "Mother's ill."

2 "The baby-sitter can only stay until 10 o'clock."

3 "The dog chews the place up if left alone too long."

4 "I must get back before the off-licence closes. Grandma will go spare if I don't collect her gin."

5 "There are so many muggings, I want to be back before dark."

6 "My last bus is at 8.30."

7 "My husband doesn't know I'm here."

8 "It gives the neighbourhood a bad reputation if I stop out late."

9 "I want to be back for the late film. I'm in it."

10 "I haven't been feeling well, but I felt I *must* come for a while."

On those very rare occasions parties are so exclusive that you don't want an excuse to get out, but a good one to get in! The following tried and trusted excuses will get you into anywhere, provided that you remember Rules 3, 7 and 10!

1 "I'm Joan Collins' latest boyfriend."

2 "Do apologise to Her Majesty for me, the Rolls broke down. I know she'll be very distraught."

3 "I'm Boy George without the make-up."

4 "I'm with Prince Andrew's party."

5 "I'm Bo Derek's younger sister."

6 "Like your features rearranged, sweetheart? Then let me in."

7 "I'm not a guest, I'm part of the cabaret."

8 "Heard of Holly Johnson? Well, I'm Frankie."

9 "I'm one of the organisers."

10 "My father built this place."

11 "I'm the surprise guest, didn't they tell you I was coming."

12 "Look, it's all very 'hush, hush', but I'm part of the 'This Is Your Life' team and we're going to spring a surprise on someone. Has Eamonn Andrews arrived yet?"

13 "I have an urgent message for one of the group, you must let me in."

14 "I'm allergic to the cold, just let me inside while we sort this out."

15 "I didn't have an invitation, I was invited over the telephone."

16 "Drug squad, let me in. Not a word to anyone."

17 "I was once an extra in 'Dynasty'."

18 "Je suis le French Ambassador's guard de body, comprendez vous, oui, oui, mon-sewer?"

19 "Sorry I'm late, but it looks bad for family to arrive first."

20 "My wife's inside, she's got the invitations."

Once inside, mingle with the crowd and enjoy yourself. Unless, of course, it happens to be one of those boring parties . . . but then you already know how to leave early!

IS YOUR JOURNEY REALLY NECESSARY?

Excuses for the Lavatory

"Is your journey really necessary?"
(RAILWAY POSTER of 1939–45 War)

When you've got to go, well you've simply got to go! But saying where and why occasionally proves embarrassing. Strange that so many euphemisms should be needed for the most natural of all bodily functions. If we're just with friends or family then we make no excuses for doing what comes naturally. Nancy Mitford readers visit the *lavatory*; 'Non-U' people go to the *toilet*; and most of us regularly nip to the *loo*. In her novel *Pride and Prejudice*, Jane Austen writes:

"On entering the drawing-room, she found the whole party at loo, and was immediately invited to join them . . ." but in the nineteenth century it meant something *quite* different!

In mixed company we may politely say that we are going to 'spend a penny', visit the 'comfort station', or, more crudely, 'shed a tear for Nelson'. It's when we're with strangers that the problems really begin, and to spare our blushes we make an excuse. A man once told his young daughter not to say that she wanted to go to the lavatory, but to say, 'I want to whisper.' One evening at a dinner party the little girl said, 'Daddy, I want to whisper,' and in front of all the guests he told her to come and do it in his ear. Remember Rule 2!

Excuse "I am going to wash my hands."
The Truth "I am going to the lavatory."

Excuse "I am just off to the Chamber of Commerce."
The Truth "I am going to the lavatory."

Excuse "I am just going to powder my nose."
The Truth "I am popping into the Gents!"

Excuse "I would like to have a look around the house."
The Truth "I want to know where the smallest room is."

Excuse "I am stopping the car, I heard a funny noise."
The Truth "I am just going to nip behind this hedge."

Excuse "Father is on the telephone at the moment."
The Truth "He is just having a tinkle upstairs."

Excuse "Mother is just changing her earrings."
The Truth "Mother had far too many cups of tea for breakfast."

Excuse "Grandfather is indisposed at the moment."
The Truth "Rhubarb always disagrees with him."

Excuse "I'm just going to get something from upstairs."
The Truth "I'm going to make a call of nature."

Excuse "I must just go and sort out the plumbing."
The Truth "I'm going to make a call of nature."

Excuse "I must just go and sort out the plumbing."
The Truth "If I don't, there will be an unexpected leak."

Being closeted in the closet can in itself be used as an excuse for:

1 Not answering the door.
2 Not answering the telephone.
3 Not switching the video on in time.
4 Keeping anyone waiting.
5 Missing the bus.
6 Being late for meals.
7 Not hearing that you are needed.
8 Not paying the milkman.
9 Avoiding carol singers.
10 Not being there when your neighbour needs a cup of sugar.

For a visit that lasts longer than anticipated and you emerge red-faced to find your impatient family waiting outside, say:

"I was just polishing the seat."

"The lock seems to jam on the door."

"I do love that new wallpaper, I could sit and look at it for hours."

WHAT BURNT BITS?

Excuses from the Kitchen

"What burnt bits? Anyway, charcoal makes your hair curl."
LADY CRABTREE

Forget Mrs Beeton, cast aside Marguerite Patten, put down Delia Smith, and completely ignore Constance Spry. They may tell you the correct way to stuff a widgeon, how many eggs you need to make zabaglione, the best time to buy neeps, and where you should stick a ratafia biscuit, but they never seem to come up with palatable excuses to explain great culinary disasters. Somehow cakes in cookery books never look like scale models of the moon's surface, sauces always thicken smoothly, meat seldom shrivels to nothing, and singed pastry is unheard of. Surely Isabella Beeton's aspic jelly didn't *always* set? Was her gravy always lumpless and did her sprouts never boil dry? She probably died at the age of

28, not through puerperal fever but at the sheer horror of discovering that her onion sauce had clotted.

All recipe books should carry a Government Health Warning so that when the lid flies off the liquidiser and you are showered in grated chocolate, or the food mixer blasts you with a cloud of self-raising flour, you are at least prepared. With new kitchen technology, excuses are needed more than ever.

WHEN:

. . . the apple pies you got out of the deep-freeze turn out to be steak and kidney:

"I do love the old-fashioned idea of a savoury course at the end of the meal, don't you?"

. . . the chocolate mousse doesn't set –
"It's a sweet soup. Lovely idea, don't you think?"

. . . the casserole doesn't taste quite right –
"I use a little known herb, it's not easy to get hold of."

. . . the pastry is black –
"But I thought you liked things well-done?"

. . . the spaghetti wouldn't fit into the saucepan –
"I like something with a bit of a crunch."

. . . you accidentally burn the meat –
"I thought we'd go vegetarian this evening."

. . . the Yorkshire pudding falls flat –
"There's something wrong with that oven."

. . . the bechamel sauce is lumpy –
"These capers don't have much taste, do they."

. . . the steak is overcooked –
"Well, if you'd been home on time."

. . . there's a slug in the salad –
"That's the meat."

. . . you've overdone the garlic –
"I don't want you kissing anyone this evening!"

... the vegetables boil dry –
"You have to let them absorb all the water, it keeps all the vitamins in."

... a boiled egg is undercooked –
"But raw eggs are good for you."

... an egg is hard-boiled –
"But I only boiled it for three minutes, it must have been too fresh."

... the pork fat doesn't get crisp –
"If you'd only give me enough housekeeping to buy a *proper* piece of pork!"

... you forgot to put the jacket potatoes in the oven –
"I like mashed potatoes the best."

... the jelly will not set –
"I thought we'd have yoghurt for pudding."

... the cream is well past the 'sell by' date –
"I do enjoy the more subtle flavour of soured cream."

... the curry is too hot –
"But vindaloo *should* be hot."

... the potatoes boil dry –
"I thought we'd have rice for a change."

... a guest asks too many questions about the ready-made dish you have palmed off as your own –
"Oh, I never give my cooking secrets away!"

... you miss out a vital ingredient –
"Sugar is very bad for you, I felt that we should try it unsweetened."

... you don't have sufficient for everyone –
"I've decided to go on a diet, but you four tuck in!"

... the vegetables are ready, but not the meat –
"Rare meat is much better for you. My great-grandfather always liked to see the blood in his meat."

... anything is burnt around the edges –
"Eat the burnt bits, they'll make your hair curl."

. . . you cannot afford a lavish meal –
"I thought you'd prefer something light."

. . . the kids complain about your meals –
"Well, I get so fed up with thinking of new things, I just go into the supermarket, kick a shelf and we have whatever falls off!"

. . . you prepare something that *you* like and nobody else does –

"Now I know you all adore this, so I prepared it specially. I've been in the kitchen all afternoon."

. . . the soup is too watery –
"I had to add more water, the vegetables were too close together."

. . . your scones fall flat –
"Have a biscuit . . ."

. . . your sponge cake fails to rise –
"But it *should* have three inches of filling in the middle."

. . . you tip in too much spice –
"This is a cinnamon cake."

. . . you misread the recipe –
"But that's what the recipe said."

. . . someone complains about your pastry *after* the meal –
"But you did remove the paper plate from underneath, didn't you?"

. . . someone breaks a tooth on your pudding –
"Great! You've found the lucky charm!"

. . . the custard will not thicken –
"Like some more clear sauce?"

. . . your hamburgers fall apart –
"Mince makes a nice change . . ."

. . . any flavour is too strong –
"I'm sure mother's scales aren't accurate."

. . . your fruit cake sinks in the middle –
"We had a power cut this morning."

. . . you drop the dish on the floor –
"Hash is so easy to make. Another spoonful?"

If you find that your family always have a lump in their
throat after your meals, always pray before they eat, and the
only thing you have for dessert is an argument, remember
that a good cook a) never admits that anything has gone
wrong; b) never hints at what the meat may be; c) calls the
soup something different every day; and d) never samples the
food first in case they don't have the nerve to dish it up!

WHAT! ALL THIS FOR A SONG?

——— Excuses from both sides of the Counter ———

"What! all this for a song?"

WILLIAM CECIL
(To Queen Elizabeth I when commanded to pay Edmund Spenser £100.)

An unkempt Arab rug pedlar was trying to sell his carpets.

'Will you buy a genuine Persian Carpet?' he asked a tourist.

'Definitely not!' exclaimed the woman, 'they stink!'

'How dare you say my carpets stink,' cried the pedlar, 'It's not them, it's me!'

People selling their own products will come up with any excuse to make you buy. Sales assistants in departmental stores, however, are another breed. The customer is never right, and if you happen to be interrupting a good gossip, they will come up with any excuse to avoid serving you or going to the stock room to get the size you want.

A manager in a well-known menswear department overheard one of the assistants say to a customer:

'No, madam, we haven't had any for a long time.'

Not wishing to lose a sale he immediately intervened.

'Yes, we have what you want, madam. I may have to order it from the warehouse, but we can certainly get it for you.'

The customer walked away laughing hysterically. Angrily he turned to the assistant.

'What did she say?' he demanded.

'All she said,' replied the assistant, 'was "we haven't had any rain lately".'

It's not just sales assistants that make excuses. If you've ever worked behind a counter you will know that customers can give far better than they get, whether it's an attempt to get their money back, or explain why they are buying a black lace bra and suspenders. Enter any large store and you'll discover a whole range of excuses being handed across the counter.

STORE GUIDE

Ground floor – Ladies fashions

Excuse "But Modom, all dresses cling that way this year."
The Truth "You're a 40 hip and we've only got a 34 in stock."

Excuse "Perhaps Modom would feel more comfortable in a slightly larger size?"
The Truth "You're much broader across the seat than I thought you were."

Excuse "Of the two, I must say that the blue suits you better."
The Truth "The blue is twenty pounds more."

Excuse "Not many people can get away with wearing red, but you can."
The Truth "You've a face like the back of a bus."

Excuse "Perhaps just a slight alteration, madam?"
The Truth "It needs three yards taken in at the waist."

Excuse "We can do alterations at only a very small cost."
The Truth "It'll be another ten quid on the price of the dress."

Excuse "These are *very* fashionable at the moment."
The Truth "It's about time these came back in fashion."

Excuse "We do have only a few left in stock."
The Truth "We've a few hundred left in stock."

Excuse "I'm afraid we don't seem to have one in your size at the moment."
The Truth "We only go up to a 54″ bust."

Excuse "Perhaps, Modom, would prefer it in pink?"
The Truth "We're trying to get rid of the pink."

Excuse "A belt is optional."
The Truth "We've lost the belt."

Excuse "A split up the side is very fashionable."
The Truth "The side seam has come undone."

Excuse "The broiderie anglais is particularly unusual."
The Truth "They haven't stitched the hem up properly."

Excuse "This frock has been worn by a queen."
The Truth "This line is very popular with transvestites."

1st floor – Millinery

Excuse "This hat is very versatile."
The Truth "You can wear it with the plastic cherries or without."

Excuse "Madam, that hat gives you height."
The Truth "You're a dumpy little thing and that feather does something for you."

Excuse "This beautiful creation would look perfect with your hairstyle."
The Truth "It will cover your hair up completely."

Excuse "Yes, our hand-knitted woollen headwear is on the display."
The Truth "There is a bobble hat in the window."

Excuse "Madam, the veil compliments your face."
The Truth "It hides your face nicely."

2nd floor – Menswear

Excuse "I'm afraid we don't have the sweater in a 40."
The Truth "I can't be bothered to go to the stockroom."

Excuse "It's fashionable to wear baggy sweaters."
The Truth "We've only got extra-large left."

Excuse "That style only comes in small, medium or large."
The Truth "I can't be bothered to hunt for an extra-large."

Excuse "If it's not on the rail we don't have it in your size."
The Truth "I can't be bothered to rummage through the rail."

Excuse "If you'd like to go through to tailoring, they'll pin the hem for you."
The Truth "Let someone else do the alteration, I'm off to lunch."

Excuse "I'm afraid we only do low-cut briefs, sir."
The Truth "I don't feel like looking through the boxer shorts."

Excuse "I think it would be much more sensible to try them on, sir."
The Truth "I want to see you without your trousers on."

Excuse "We only go up to a 16½ collar, I'm afraid."
The Truth "I'm not climbing to the top shelf for a 17."

Excuse "It's the French sizes, they come up slightly larger."
The Truth "We converted the metric size wrongly."

3rd floor – Pharmacy

Excuse "Can I collect my prescription when you are less busy?"
The Truth "I've got VD and don't want everyone to know."

Excuse "Do you have a mild antiseptic ointment for gnat bites?"
The Truth "I've got piles."

Excuse "Do you keep flea powder – it's for the dog."
The Truth "My husband's got lice."

Excuse "Can you recommend something for a slight rash?"
The Truth "I've got an embarrassing itch."

4th floor – Electrical repairs

Excuse "We are waiting for a part."
The Truth "We haven't looked at it yet."

Excuse "It is not worthwhile repairing."
The Truth "We'd rather sell you a new one."

Excuse "It will look as good as new."
The Truth "You'll always see the join."

Excuse "The replacement parts are quite expensive."
The Truth "The part will cost more than the machine did originally."

Excuse "We have an expert looking at it."
The Truth "We couldn't do it ourselves."

Excuse "We had to give it a completely new part."
The Truth "We only soldered two wires together."

5th floor – Hairdressing salon

Excuse "This style would make you look much younger."
The Truth "This style is ten pounds more than a wash-and-set."

Excuse "It's the modern look."
The Truth "The perm went wrong."

Excuse "But green hair is very fashionable today."
The Truth "It was meant to be blonde, so what?"

Excuse "The conditioner is expensive, but it will cure your split ends."
The Truth "I'll cut off the split ends, so you'll think it's worked."

Excuse "Yes, some of the hair will fall out, it's quite normal."
The Truth "The bleach was left on too long."

Excuse "It's static electricity."
The Truth "It's been badly cut."

Excuse "It's not quite as you wanted, but your hair was too fine for a 'Princess Diana' look."
The Truth "I couldn't be bothered to layer it."

NO MAN IS A BORN ANGLER

Sporting Excuses

> *"As no man is born an artist, so no man is born an angler."*
> IZAAK WALTON

A keen game shooter was standing in the butchers.
'No, I'm sorry sir,' said the butcher, 'we don't have any wild duck, but we do have some lovely plump chickens.'
'Don't be silly,' said the sportsman, 'I can't go home and tell my wife that I shot a chicken!'

Whatever the sport, you can be certain that there will be something foul somewhere. The golfer who misses a birdie, the angler who catches a tiddler, the cricketer that drops a catch, the jockey that comes in so late that he has to creep past the other stables so as not to wake the horses, the gambler with an extra ace up his sleeve, they all get the highest score when it comes to making excuses.

We would have won, but:

1 "The pitch was too wet."

2 "I lost a contact lens just as I went for the penalty."

3 "It was a new ball, we weren't used to it."

4 "We had to bring on the substitute. He was useless."

5 "We never get on so well when we're playing away from home."

6 "I had new studs on my boots, they need running in."

7 "We had the sun in our eyes in the second half."

8 "I've never been the same since my cartilage operation."

9 "The referee was biased."

10 "The crowd were distracting. Hooligans, the lot of them."

Sorry, love, I didn't catch anything today:

1 "It was too cold for them to come out."

2 "The river's so polluted that I don't think there's anything in it."

3 "The fish was so big it broke the line and got away."

4 "They don't seem to like maggots like they used to."

5 "Those worms you dug up for me were useless."

6 "That new rod just isn't the same."

7 "Too many noisy kids around the water, frightened them all off."

8 "Some cat came and ate the bait."

9 "I didn't feel like it today."

10 "They gnawed through the line. Getting crafty these days, you know."

Far worse than actually losing at your sport is being in the position that you *almost* won. Whatever your game, be it hockey, pigeon shooting or tiddly-winks, here are the Top Twenty excuses to explain why you didn't quite win.

1 "The wind was in the wrong direction."

2 "My foot slipped."

3 "I think I pulled a muscle in my back."

4 "The birds sat coughing in the trees."

5 "The elastic in my shorts came loose. It put me off."

6 "I was exhausted after the pre-match shower."

7 "Smoke got in my eyes."

8 "I suffer from nerves."

9 "Someone coughed at the wrong moment."

10 "I've been training too hard. Knocked myself out before the game."

11 "I think someone spiked my drink."

12 "I didn't trust the guy behind me. Keeping an eye on him, I missed the ball."

13 "The horse was too frisky."

14 "My equipment came to pieces."

15 "The scorer cheated."

16 "I forgot the rules of the game."

17 "I should never have had sex before the game."

18 "All the other players were on drugs.

19 "I deliberately let the other side/person win."

20 "I could have done better, I just wasn't trying that's all."

If you are the kind of sportsman that gets tired just lifting a ping-pong ball, you don't need excuses to explain defeat, but to avoid playing altogether. To get out of sports simply blame:

1. Weak ankles.
2. Housemaids knee.
3. Limp wrists.
4. Old war wounds.
5. High blood pressure.
6. Possible pregnancy.
7. Allergy to the weather.
8. All year round hayfever.
9. Lack of practice.
10. Broken glasses.

WOT ME? IN MY STATE OF HEALTH?

————— Medical Excuses —————

"Wot, me? In my state of health!"
TED KAVANAGH (Itma programmes)

Of all the excuses that we make feigned illness comes right at the top of the list. The bad back excuse can get you out of practically anything, the headache excuse can prevent you getting in to anything, and the upset stomach excuse never fails to get you a day off work. As 'sick' excuses have been around since God was a little boy, it is now wise to produce a really credible illness to arouse as much sympathy as possible. Preferably nothing fatal, but you can always have 'acute nasopharyngitis' (a common cold) or 'allergic rhinitis' (hay fever).

A man who went deaf suddenly was told by his doctor that it

was the result of too much alcohol, so he cut out the drink and his hearing returned. Six weeks later he was back in the surgery.

'No wonder you've gone deaf again,' shouted the doctor, 'you're back on the bottle, aren't you!'

'Ah, well, doctor,' replied the patient, hastily thinking of a good excuse, 'you see, I liked what I was drinking much better than what I was hearing.'

It's not only patients that make excuses, but doctors are even bigger culprits when they cannot explain what is wrong with you. One doctor told a patient that he'd got 'Alice'. He didn't know what it was, but Christopher Robin went down with it! If you think that your GP might be equally incompetent, never be fooled by the following common excuses:

Excuse "I'm going to refer you to Dr Brown."
The Truth "I don't know what the hell you've got."

Excuse "I'm going to send you for tests."
The Truth "I can't be bothered to waste time on you."

Excuse "I can't do anything until the condition gets worse."
The Truth "That'll get rid of you for the next six months."

Excuse "This prescription will cure you in no time."
The Truth "When you discover the prescription charges you'll soon stop pestering me!"

Excuse "I think it's only a strained muscle."
The Truth "Well, it's the cause of most aches and pains."

Excuse "I'm afraid the doctor is away on an urgent call at the moment."
The Truth "If he doesn't win this round of golf he'll never get through to the Surgeons' and Orthopaedist's Classic."

Excuse "I only specialise in the ears and throat."
The Truth "I don't feel like looking up your nose today."

Excuse "I'm going to send you to a venereologist."
The Truth "I'm not going to risk catching herpes."

If the doctor is too busy to see you (Remember that appointments must be booked three weeks in advance) the friendly receptionist is always more than willing to tell you where to go:

1 "It looks like a wart to me, go away!"

2 "The doctor has patients with far more serious problems, crawl home."

3 "We're still waiting for the results of your test, ring us in June."

4 "We've lost your medical records."

5 "You can't drip blood all over the floor in here, go somewhere else."

6 "There are no appointments left."

7 "You can't come in here, spreading your nasty germs about like that."

8 "The doctor's off sick."

9 "It's one minute past eleven, sorry, surgery ended at eleven o'clock. Come back tomorrow."

10 "The doctor can only see emergency cases. I don't consider smallpox to be an emergency."

Being a doctor has many compensations. You can double-park where you like; get anyone to strip naked *and* send them a bill for it, and you never have to apologise for illegible handwriting. A doctor, however, cannot get a day off work with a medical excuse because he's supposed to know how to cure it! This is where ordinary mortals have the advantage.

I can't because:

1 "I've just been bitten by the dog. I'm about to go for a rabies jab."

2 "I've been spitting blood all morning, I don't suppose it's anything serious."

3 "It's the wrong time of the month."

4 "I'm on diuretics; I can't drive anywhere without having to stop every five minutes."

5 "I've twisted my ankle, I can't even let my foot touch the floor."

6 "I think it might be mumps, my glands are really swollen."

7 "I keep getting these dizzy spells, it must be my age."

8 "I can't remember what you call it, but the doctor says it's highly contagious."

9 "We've all got Bubonic plague."

10 "We've all got terrible food poisoning. I knew Brenda should never have gone into the woods for those mushrooms."

CABBAGE WITH A COLLEGE EDUCATION

Excuses in the Restaurant

"Cauliflower is nothing but cabbage with a college education."
MARK TWAIN

The domestic cook serves up a culinary disaster with an excuse; the professional chef gives it a foreign name and leaves the excuses to the waiter. Most restaurants should be awarded a cordon bleu certificate for cooking up better excuses than meals. Any waiter worth his salt will know the classic ones to explain the fly in the soup ("That's not a fly, it's the meat.") but the really efficient have taken the advance course.

Excuse "Continental food is our speciality."
The Truth "We just throw everything together and call it something fancy."

Excuse "Ours is high-class cuisine for the gourmet."
The Truth "We charge twice as much as everybody else, so diners think it *must* be good."

Excuse "I will choose the wine to accompany your meal."
The Truth "I will choose the most expensive wine."

Excuse "The Prince of Wales always drinks the Bollinger '75."
The Truth "We've got two cases we want to shift."

Excuse "May I recommend the duck?"
The Truth "That duck will never keep another day."

Excuse "The chef has flambéd your steak, madam."
The Truth "It caught fire under the grill."

Excuse "The ragout is particularly piquant."
The Truth "The chef overdid the tabasco sauce."

Excuse "I don't know what the soup of the day is."
The Truth "The label came off the tin, nobody knows what is."

Excuse "But the vegetables *are* fresh, sir."
The Truth "I took them fresh from the freezer myself."

What do you mean 'it tastes odd'?

1 "It's just our own unique delicate blend of herbs and spices."

2 "It's the chef's own unique recipe."

3 "It must be your taste buds, sir, nobody else has complained."

4 "That's how tripe should taste."

5 "I expect you misread the menu."

6 "That's what you ordered, that's what you've got."

7 "I can do nothing about it now you've started eating it."

8 "It should have been eaten immediately, otherwise the flavour is impaired."

9 "But the truffles are the very best, I don't expect you've ever had them fresh before."

10 "It's not my fault, I only laid the table."

What do you mean 'the bill's too steep'?

1 "This *is* Knightsbridge, sir."

2 "It does include VAT and service."

3 "It does say a minimum charge of £50 if you read the small print at the bottom of the menu, sir."

4 "Our chef is ex-Buckingham Palace."

5 "Silly me, I've given you the Getty's bill by mistake."

6 "I've put an extra nought in by mistake, slip of the pen."

7 "But the wine was £150 a bottle, did I not tell you?"

8 "It was because you ordered *fresh* asparagus. It's not the season you see."

9 "We are recommended by Egon Ronay."

10 "We have to pay the staff triple time after nine o'clock."

As you would expect, we diners are just as bad. Some people can never bring themselves to say what they really mean!

Excuse "Can you recommend a local restaurant?"
The Truth "Is there somewhere cheap nearby?"

Excuse "You can't come, I'm going with the boss to an exclusive restaurant."
The Truth "We're going to a Soho strip club."

Excuse "I never eat in cheap restaurants, they're so common."
The Truth "All my meals go down on the firm's expense account."

Excuse "I'm not really very hungry this evening, let's have a pizza."
The Truth "Have you seen the prices on the menu!"

Excuse "I won't have any dessert, but you have some."
The Truth "I can't afford to pay for two."

Excuse "That place looks too crowded, let's go somewhere more informal."
The Truth "I'm not paying those prices, let's go to the Wimpy."

NECESSITY'S SHARP PINCH

Financial Excuses

"Necessity's sharp pinch!"
SHAKESPEARE (King Lear)

If you try to make as much money as you can, people call you materialistic. If you keep it, you're a capitalist. Spend it and you're branded a playboy. Earn a comfortable wage and you're said to lack drive. Go on the dole and you're branded a parasite. Slave away and save for a happy retirement, and you're accused of being a fool that's wasted his life. In other words, wherever money is concerned you simply cannot win!

There is a Russian proverb that says, 'No man will ever be hanged if he has money in his pocket', and refute it though we try, nobody can deny that money talks. When Winston Churchill was Prime Minister, he was one evening on his way to the BBC to make a speech. He hailed a taxi and asked the driver to take him to Broadcasting House.

'I'm sorry, guv, I can't go that far tonight.'

'Why ever not,' demanded the Prime Minister, 'why can't you take me to the BBC?'

'Well, mate, Mr Churchill's on the wireless in half an hour, and I must get home to hear him.'

Churchill smiled to himself and produced a pound note (at a time when the pound *was* a note and worth something!) and held it towards the cabbie.

'Hop in, sir,' said the driver, 'Who gives a damn about Mr Churchill!'

Money, money, money . . . with it, or without it, we somehow always need a golden excuse.

Excuses for being in debt:

1 "My wife ran off with my bank manager."

2 "The dog chewed up my wallet. Money, credit cards, everything's gone."

3 "My dole cheque blew away."

4 "It's my husband, he drinks."

5 "The kid's fees at Eton went up this year."

6 "The share prices have fallen."

7 "I invested all my capital in De Lorean."

8 "The gas bill came at the same time as the roof caved in."

9 "The Inland Revenue just do not understand my situation."

10 "I pay my ex-wives so much in maintenance that I cannot even afford to eat."

There are *rare* occasions when we have to account for having more money than we should have. Especially when partners dust your wallet and accidentally discover that little extra!

1 "Just a little sweepstake amongst the girls at work. I struck lucky, that's all."

2 "I've been saving for your birthday present."

3 "I've been selling my body again." (Chuckle, then change the subject).

4 "There was too much in my wage packet. Shhh, don't tell anyone."

5 "Only a small tax rebate, goodness knows I pay them enough."

6 "I found some in my old suit. It must have been there months."

7 "I sold one of my grandfather's medals; I didn't want you to go short."

8 "A colleague returned some cash I lent him, that's all."

9 "It was the Millionaire's Bingo, but I didn't quite win."

10 "It's just some money I had for my birthday, of course I haven't had a pay rise without telling you."

I AM NOT ARGUING WITH YOU

Excuses on the Road

"I am not arguing with you, I am telling you!"
WHISTLER

The day after passing their driving test, most drivers forget the Highway Code and begin to learn the true rules of the road:

a The other driver is always in the wrong.
b The fastest car has the right of way.
c Park anywhere as long as you don't get caught.
d He who is stopped by the police can never speak English.
e Always slow down when passing a red light.
f If forced to park at a meter, stop where you have the choice of two.
g If in doubt, blame the guy that sold you the car.
h He who shouts the loudest gets the insurance money.

It was a writer called Christopher North who at the beginning of the nineteenth century first expressed the sentiment that laws are made to be broken. The ebullient Mae West, a law unto herself, was not of the same mind. Laws should *not* be broken, but it didn't matter, she once said, if you cracked them just a little! All drivers break the law at some time, be it the vicar that drives like Jehu (see 2 Kings 9:20 'The driving is like the driving of Jehu, the son of Nimshi; for he driveth furiously'!) or the old admiral who emulates Nelson ('I have a right to be blind sometimes . . . I really do not see the signal.'), but anyone can get away with it providing they steer excuses in the right direction.

I'm sorry, officer, but:

1 "I couldn't see through the windscreen for all the road safety stickers."

2 "We were all in the back seat at the time."

3 "It looked like a body in the road, so I swerved to avoid it."

4 "I'm very low on petrol, so I was getting home as quickly as I could before it ran out."

5 "But this car won't do more than 70."

6 "I was on my way to the police station to report an accident."

7 "The accelerator sticks on this car, I was just driving to the garage to get it seen to."

8 "There was a naked girl hitch-hiking, would you have kept your eyes on the road?"

9 "I was teaching my wife to drive and was demonstrating what happens if you don't know your left from your right."

10 "It was her fault! She pushed her shopping trolley straight under the wheels of my car."

It is not only the police that hear excuses on the road, but also the insurance companies who have to decide whether truth is stranger than fiction when assessing your claim. No accident is ever your fault!

Excuse "The accident was due to the other man narrowly missing me."
The Truth "Unfortunately I didn't narrowly miss him."

Excuse "The road was slippery and I skidded."
The Truth "I was drunk."

Excuse "It was a mechanical fault in the car."
The Truth "Caused by the nut behind the wheel."

Excuse "The other man must have been to blame."
The Truth "I was too drunk to have done anything like that."

Excuse "I think it was an act of God."
The Truth "If God hadn't invented cars I would never have had the accident."

Excuse "It was the fault of the council."
The Truth "They put up the fence that I drove through."

An Insurance company who happened to represent both parties involved in a minor car accident, was unable to reach a satisfactory conclusion as to the cause of the accident. In the end they agreed that it was 'An act of God, under very suspicious circumstances.' Before requiring excuses to explain your behaviour on the road, you need first to have a vehicle. Fortunately today the stereo-typed 'Honest Joe' second-hand car salesman has been forced to take a back seat. Now you need much more sophisticated excuses to encourage motorists to buy a car.

1 "All modern cars come complete with a bucket of left-over parts."

2 "That's not a scratch, it's a sleek line down the side of the bodywork. All deluxe models have it."

3 "Oh, odd hub caps are very much in vogue."

4 "Cobwebs in the engine proves that it never needs anything doing to it."

5 "Yes, the log book is written in Portuguese, it's part of the car's curiosity value."

6 "We have changed the number plates. The previous owner was very attached to them."

7 "No, that isn't rust, it's the subtle mottled effect of the paintwork."

8 "The knocking in the engine is deliberate. It makes your car stand out in a crowd, and you'll always know when your husband's coming home."

9 "It's very economical. It only uses oil when the engine's running."

10 "The wing mirrors are loose. That means you can lock them inside the car to prevent theft."

BLESSED IS HE WHO EXPECTS NOTHING

Travel Excuses

"Blessed is he who expects nothing, for he shall never be disappointed."
ALEXANDER POPE

'Travelling,' wrote Thomas Jefferson, 'makes men wiser, but less happy.' Wiser, because as the years go by we come to terms with the fact that we will never arrive anywhere on time. Less happy, because we know that the reasons given for delays are nothing but excuses. In the summer trains are late because the tracks expand with the heat; in autumn there are 'leaves on the line'; there are severe delays in winter because of 'adverse weather conditions', and as the new financial year approaches in the spring it is a time for industrial action and rail strikes to secure higher wages.

I once sat in a railway carriage on one of those frustrating occasions when the train departs at the precise second that it should, and foolishly your spirits rise with renewed faith until suddenly you stop inexplicably in no-man's-land for twenty-five minutes. The other passengers in my compartment started discussing just why they thought the railways were losing so much money. One young man said it was all due to faulty management, another said it was laziness on the part of the staff, and a woman put it down to the fact that too many people were employed. A second woman was just about to air her views when they heard the ticket inspector coming and they all dived under the seats!

For passengers that can afford a second mortgage to buy a train ticket, it would be so much fairer if British Rail issued a free guide to their announcements as part of their new friendly approach!

Excuse "The train on platform ten to Plymouth will leave approximately thirty minutes late due to earlier signal failure."
The Truth "The driver overslept again."

Excuse "We regret the late arrival of your train, this was due to engineering works on the line."
The Truth "The driver missed his bus to work."

Excuse "British Rail regret the 19.06 train to Liverpool has been cancelled."
The Truth "The driver's wife doesn't like him working overtime."

Excuse "The late arrival of the 9.26 train to Ipswich was because of signal failure."
The Truth "Some silly bugger forgot to change them."

Excuse "Will passengers to Southend travel in the front four coaches."
The Truth "The ticket collector will not have to walk the full length of the train."

Excuse "Will passengers on platform one please note that the 8.26 to King's Cross will now leave from platform eighteen."

The Truth "The 8.26 has been cancelled, but by the time you've puffed your way to platform eighteen, you'll think it's gone."

It isn't only poor British Rail who try and ease our fevered brows with excuses. The airlines make their fair share too . . .

Excuse "Flight 2708 to Brussels has been delayed by two hours owing to adverse weather conditions."
The Truth "It's raining and the stewardess doesn't want to get her hair wet crossing the tarmac."

Excuse "The flights to New York have been cancelled until further notice."
The Truth "The rate of the dollar is about to change, if we wait we can increase the fares."

Excuse "I'm afraid you'll have to pay excess baggage."
The Truth "Your wife is overweight."

Excuse "We are encountering slight turbulence, please fasten your seat belts."
The Truth "The pilot has had too much duty free scotch again."

Excuse "We will be landing at De Gaulle airport to refuel."
The Truth "The pilot's French mistress is waiting for him."

Excuse "Our beautiful air hostesses are here to cater for your every need."
The Truth "For some needs you'll require either Visa or American Express."

Before you even set out, your friendly travel agent will make every excuse in the book to get as much money as possible out of you. Somehow there are certain phrases which never appear in the travel guides . . .

Excuse "We would advise that you fly from Gatwick."
The Truth "It would be quicker and cheaper from Heathrow, but we can charge you extra for the coach."

Excuse "It is advisable to book in January to be sure of the best holiday."
The Truth "We can then have eleven months rest, and charge everyone else an extra supplement for booking late."

Excuse "It is a beautiful city, you cannot hope to see everything in less than a fortnight."
The Truth "The mean old trout was only going to have ten days."

Excuse "I'm afraid we can only offer you two single rooms in the hotel of your choice."
The Truth "There are plenty of doubles, but singles cost extra."

Excuse "The luxury holiday motel has self-catering facilities."
The Truth "You've got to buy your own food."

Where travel is concerned, the people that hear the most excuses are the men from Her Majesty's Customs and Excise. When Oscar Wilde walked through customs on his arrival in New York, he announced: 'I have nothing to declare, except my genius.' Some travellers have so much more . . .

Excuse "I always wear two watches so that I can keep track of the time difference."
The Truth "I hope you won't notice the other eighteen up my sleeve."

Excuse "I've got two bottles of whiskey to declare."
The Truth "As long as I declare something, you won't notice the other four bottles in my suitcase."

Excuse "This is purely for my personal use."
The Truth "I intend to sell it just as soon as I get home."

Excuse "It is already opened."
The Truth "I opened them all so that you can't charge me duty on them."

Excuse "I'm awfully sorry. I didn't know the regulations."
The Truth "I did know the regulations, I hoped I wouldn't get caught."

Excuse "I had all my money stolen abroad."
The Truth "I'm going to avoid paying duty if it's the last thing I do."

Excuse "I've lost the keys to this bag."
The Truth "You're not going to look inside."

Excuse "I took both these cameras with me."
The Truth "I bought one of them abroad."

Excuse "No, no, it's for medical reasons. My doctor insists."
The Truth "It's pure alcohol, my doctor insists I give it up."

DAYS OF WINE AND ROSES

—— Forgotten Anniversary Excuses ——

"They are not long, the days of wine and roses."
ERNEST DOWSON

When a husband suddenly finds his bedroom door locked from the inside, his sandwiches wrapped in a roadmap, and ground glass at the bottom of his coffee cup, it can only mean one thing. Either he has forgotten his wife's birthday, or it's their wedding anniversary. As women hate to be reminded about their age ('saving money are you, darling? Only 29 candles on the cake . . .') and men try hard to forget that they're married ('I want to give chocolates to the girl I love, but my wife won't let me . . .'), it's hardly surprising. The best way to remember an anniversary is to forget it *once*!

It's not too late to save the day if you can come up with a

pacifying excuse before the end of it. Forget the date altogether and you could be crawling all the way to the divorce court.

I haven't really forgotten, sweetheart:

1 "I knew you'd have so many presents today that I thought it would be nice to spread out the celebration and give you my gift on Friday."

2 "But you did say that you didn't want to be reminded about your 50th birthday, so I didn't remind you."

3 "You said 'Don't get me anything expensive', so I didn't."

4 "You mean it *didn't* arrive in the post? I thought you were just too overcome with emotion to mention it."

5 "Oh, you've cooked dinner already, and I was going to take you out to supper as a surprise. What a pity this salad won't keep."

6 "But surely it's tomorrow . . ."

7 "I bought you an emerald ring, then I suddenly remembered that green is your unlucky colour so I took it back."

8 "I've ordered two dozen of your favourite flowers. Unfortunately they won't be here until Belladonna's back in season."

9 "My love for you is priceless. So I didn't buy you anything. I thought we'd have an early night."

10 "But you had a birthday *last* year!"

As a final resort, look her straight in the bi-focals, prise the carving knife from her fingers, and give the biggest smile you can muster as you say:
    'But *every day* with you is a celebration, my sweet, why should today be any different?'
If that fails, pray.

When a couple have lived together for over twenty years the

most romantic evening is when they both stay in and argue over which TV programme to watch. A wedding anniversary does provide a welcome excuse to be nice to each other, just for once. But I wonder if even then couples say what they really mean . . .

Her: "You remembered our anniversary, darling, how sweet."
– If you'd forgotten again I would have killed you.

Him: "But of course I remembered, my sweet."
– Thank God the kids reminded me.

Her: "Twenty-three happy years together."
– Twenty three years of hell.

Him: "I could never forget our wedding, cherub."
– How can you forget the worst day of your life?

Him: "It only seems like yesterday that I proposed to you."
– I wish it was yesterday, I needn't turn up at the wedding.

Her: "Darling, this lovely present is exactly what I wanted."
– It ought to be, I've dropped enough bloody hints.

Him: "I thought we'd go back to the restaurant where I proposed to you."
– I'm dying to go back, they've got topless waitresses now.

Her: "I'd rather not, I'd like to remember it as it was."
– I'm not going back there, they've got topless waitresses now.

Him: "Perhaps you're right, dearest."
– Who wants to be reminded of one's mistakes anyway.

Her: "Let's have a quiet evening in together."
– Let's see if we can get through just one night without an argument.

Him: "It's occasions like this that bring romantic memories flooding back."
– I wonder what happened to Gloria Mountshaft with the big . . .

Should the ultimate disaster occur, and you forget *your*

mother's birthday, parental bonds need not be totally severed! Blame:

The Post Office
Jet Lag
The Florist
The Government
Delivery Boys

Telephone and say:
"We're planning a big surprise for you at the weekend."

If all else fails, flattery won't:

"But mother, you still only look forty. I thought you'd stopped having birthdays ages ago!"

CUT HER THROAT BUT PERSUADE HER!

Excuses to get rid of Doorstep Salesmen

"Persuade her. Cut her throat but persuade her!"
JOE ORTON (Entertaining Mr Sloane)

The true art of being a salesman is to convince the would-be buyer that life will be intolerable without the product on offer. Whether it's a complete set of encyclopaedias or a set of lavatory brushes, door-to-door salesmen are the masters of persuasion. It is easier to prise a limpet off a rock, or lure a man away from Joan Collins, than it is to push the foot of a salesman away from your door. Many buy just *one* encyclopaedia to prop up a leg of the bed, or the smallest squirrel-hair paintbrush, simply to appease the persistent commission-seeking intruder.

My favourite story is of the elderly lady who purchased a

lavatory brush just to be free of a doorstep salesman. Considering her to be any easy target, the man called back a few months later, and his first question was naturally about the brush.

'Oh, I can't buy another one,' said the lady, 'I like it very much, but it's my husband. He can't cope with the bristles and says he's going to stick to toilet paper."

The doorstep salesman's manual is packed with excuses to encourage you to buy:

1 "You won't find one cheaper."

2 "It's the latest model."

3 "I'm quoting this price to you as a very special favour."

4 "You won't find one like it anywhere."

5 "All your neighbours have just bought one."

6 "You'll regret it in a few months time when you're the only one without."

7 "These are the genuine article, none of your foreign rubbish."

8 "The price is going up next week."

9 "My wife wouldn't be without one."

10 "I don't know how you've managed so long without one, this will save you hours."

To avoid being duped, ignore the sales patter, forget the impressive packaging, and remember that if something appears to be a bargain someone is going to be cheated, and it is *never* the salesman! If a product is worth having, you will go out and buy it, it doesn't need to make its own way to your door. Next time there is an unexpected knock, be ready with your own line of sales chat . . .

1 "We've already got one."

2 "My husband owns the company."

3 "We were the first in the street to have double glazing."

4 "You'll have to ask my husband, he's just polishing his truncheon."

5 "Don't come any further, we've all got cholera." (Through the letter box.)

6 "No thank you, but I've just patented this new anti-mugging spray, can I give you a demonstration?"

7 "My husband's at a meeting with Sinn Fein, can I get him to call on you?"

8 "Oh are those *still* on the market! I had a job like yours twenty years ago. Depressing, isn't it!"

9 "I can't stop, I think the dog's got rabies. You couldn't come in and hold him while I call the vet?"

10 "Useless, I've tried it. I prefer embalming fluid."

FATHER IS RATHER VULGAR, MY DEAR

Excuses for the Children

> *"Father is rather vulgar, my dear. The word Papa, besides, gives a pretty form to the lips. Papa, potatoes, poultry, prunes and prism, are all very good words for the lips: especially prunes and prism."*
>
> CHARLES DICKENS (Mrs General in 'Little Dorrit')

The life of a child is made up of excuses. If we're not making excuses *to* them or *for* them, they are making excuses to us! The greatest embarrassment occurs when the little dears start to discover their own anatomy, and we have to make excuses to stop them doing what comes naturally.

'Don't touch, it will drop off!'
'You'll go blind!'
'Daddy will be cross!'
'It's wicked, God will punish you!'

flushed mother's used to cry, hastily reaching for a copy of *Winnie the Pooh* to change the subject.

A little boy was once asking his mother about the facts of life.
  'Mummy, where did I come from?' he demanded.
  'Well, dear, the stork brought you.'
  'Then where did you come from?'
  'Oh,' blushed the embarrassed mother, 'I was found under a gooseberry bush.'
  'And what about grandpa, where did he come from?'
  'Grandpa was left on a doorstep by the fairies,' gushed the mother, 'Now, no more questions, get on with your homework.'
The little boy settled down to his biology and wrote:
  'There have been no natural births in our family for at least three generations.'

Parents, quite naturally, always think that their own child is perfect. Someone once defined a 'brat' as a child that behaves like your own, but belongs to someone else. Trying not to offend doting mothers and proud fathers can lead to excuses galore when it comes to writing school reports. Leopold Godowsky, a noted American pianist, once had the formidable task of teaching a clumsy, tone-deaf and totally unmusical child to play the piano. The parents kept demanding a progress report, and the embarrassed musician continued evading the truth and made excuses. Eventually Godowsky was pressured into putting something concrete in writing. He wrote: 'Your daughter is not without lack of talent, and she manages to play the simplest pieces with the greatest of difficulty.'

Now look at your infant prodigy's report with open eyes – if only all head teachers annotated the text!

"Fiona's work has reached the expected level."
(We didn't expect much of her.)

"Michael continues to work with his usual enthusiasm."
(He still hates everybody.)

"Millicent has a slight communication problem with children
of her own peer group."
(She just won't stop hitting them.)

"Adrian is still slightly behind with his reading skills."
(At 17 it's time he learnt to read!)

"Julian is extremely fond of the weekly Physical Exercise
period."
(He likes playing with the other boys in the showers.)

"We have encountered some problems with Barry this term."
(He never attends lessons, we don't know who he is.)

"Cynthia is very keen to obtain her woodwork 'A' level,"
(The staff are convinced that Cynthia is a lesbian.)

"Kenneth's unusual social habits do give some cause for
concern."
(We wish Kenneth wouldn't play with himself under the
desk.)

"Brian's work does leave a little to be desired."
(We wish he would do some.)

"Monica has a very comprehensive vocabulary for her age."
(She can swear in Latin and French.)

"Susan has a very big future ahead of her."
(If she still intends to run her own brothel when she leaves
school.)

"Malcolm particularly enjoys outdoor activities."
(He keeps being discovered behind the bicycle sheds.)

"Your son is top in biology."
(He is sexually advanced for his age.)

"Satisfactory progress."
(He manages to keep awake now.)

"Quite good."
(She comes to school at least three days a week.)

"Good."
(His work is excellent, but we don't want it to go to his head.)

"Excellent."
(The staff are having problems keeping up with him.)

"We expect Peter to do well in his 'O' levels."
(If he cheats like he did in the mock exams.)

Few children need excuses made on their behalf, they are quite capable of making them for themselves. Walking through Hyde Park recently I saw a group of youngsters throwing sticks at a frightened cat perched precariously in a tree.

'Don't worry, mister,' shouted one of the boys. 'We're only trying to coax it down so that we can stroke it.'

Today children seem to know all the answers:

"I'm not poking the baby, I'm counting his measles."

"If Daddy can do it, so can I."

"The catapult went off when I wasn't looking."

Oh, yes, youth really is wasted on the young!

TO THINE OWN SELF BE TRUE

How to Deceive Yourself

> *"This above all; to thine own self be true,*
> *And it must follow, as the night the day,*
> *Thou canst not then be false to any man."*
> SHAKESPEARE (Hamlet)

'We are only falsehood, duplicity, contradiction;' wrote Pascal in 1670, 'we both conceal and disguise ourselves from ourselves.' Over three hundred years later evolution has done little to alter this self-deceiving trait in human nature, but then if evolution worked we all would have had three pairs of hands years ago.

Man is the only animal that makes excuses. Monkeys never feel the need to justify the theft of another ape's banana; it's the law of the jungle that the lion gets his share even though it's the lioness whose been slaving over a hot plain all morning preparing a juicy wildebeest; and even if dogs had the ability, it is unlikely that any self-respecting hound would blame a leaking radiator for his puddle on the floor. Even less probable is the suggestion that animals make any attempt to deceive themselves, but who can tell? May be elephants have no qualms about tucking into sticky buns, thinking:

'I can soon jog off half-a-ton this afternoon.'

Perhaps the rhino feels that it isn't ugly, but sees a distorted reflection in the swamp water and blames that, and possibly the overweight gorilla simply lolls on its back, pats its fat belly and sighs: 'I can't do anything about it, it runs in the family.'

If animals don't make excuses to themselves, human beings more than make up for it!

I'm not really overweight:

1 "*All* my family are high-waisted."

2 "I've been exercising, this is muscle not fat."

3 "This frock is so old, it's been going at the seams for ages."

4 "The bathroom scales are wrong."

5 "The shape of your body changes as you get older."

6 "It's only because you're so thin that I look fat."

7 "Anyway, I need sugar to give me energy."

8 "It's water, the doctor's given me some pills."

9 "I'm on a carbohydrate and starch diet."

10 "It's just this chunky sweater I'm wearing."

The worst time of life is that awful period between forty and sixty. You're not young enough to do all the things you used to, and not decrepit enough to use old age as an excuse. Your mind still says 'Go, go, go', but your body's screaming 'No, no, no.' People say that you look like a million, and you feel every year of it, then the kids say that they can tell your age by counting the rings around your eyes. Little wonder that many suffer a mid-life crisis! It's when reaching maturity that we really begin to make excuses to ourselves . . .

Excuse "They don't make clothes as well as they used to."
The Truth "It's middle-aged spread."

Excuse "I think a high neckline suits me."
The Truth "It doesn't reveal my scraggy neck."

Excuse "I always eat bran, it keeps me going."
The Truth "Is constipation a sign of age?"

Excuse "They don't put as much hair colour in a bottle as they used to."
The Truth "I've got more grey hairs than I used to have."

Excuse "Grey hairs make a woman look dignified."
The Truth "They make you look old."

Excuse "The odd wrinkle gives my face character."
The Truth "My face looks like a road map."

Excuse "A few lines show that I have lived."
The Truth "I look as if I've lived a double life."

Excuse "The little bump on my nose is part of me, it makes me unique."
The Truth "I've got a damn great hooter, and I hate it."

Excuse "Men prefer the plumper woman, they like something to get hold of."
The Truth "I'm bloody fat and if he doesn't like it, he'll just have to lump it!"

Excuse "I don't find it quite so easy to touch my toes."
The Truth "I haven't even seen my feet for years!"

Excuse "I think long hair suits me."
The Truth "I look like a yeti, but I can't afford to have it cut."

Excuse "I'm now a mature and sophisticated woman."
The Truth "Just face facts Vera, you're getting old!"

Beauty is in the eye of the beholder, but if you don't behold yourself to be beautiful then there must be someone you can blame:

1 "It's my mother's fault, all her family have big hips."

2 "I was alright until I had the children."

3 "It's my wife's fault, she sleeps on me at night."

4 "I was hit by a bus, what's your excuse?"

5 "I blame the blitz myself."

6 "Winklepickers, ruined my posture they did."

7 "My silicone implants rejected me."

8 "Those holidays in the Bahamas caused premature ageing."

IF CLEOPATRA'S NOSE HAD BEEN SHORTER

— Emergency Excuses —

"If Cleopatra's nose had been shorter, the whole face of the earth would have changed."

BLAISE PASCAL

There are times when you desperately need an excuse, it doesn't matter what it is, but you must have one. You knock in a nail to hang a picture and suddenly find yourself in next door's sitting-room; a naturalist's car breaks down and you immediately have to explain to the wife just why you are underneath a Volvo with a naked blonde; the telephone engineer gets an electric shock and your husband arrives home as you are giving him the kiss of life. Help! Scream! Panic!

To save your skin, reach out for an excuse. Here are 101

random excuses for you to clutch at in your hour of need . . .

101 "It was the dog's fault."

100 "The telephone rang just at the wrong moment."

99 "I didn't even touch it, it just came to pieces in my hand."

98 "The clock stopped."

97 "It's never been the same since North Sea Gas."

96 "The cat's been sick on the carpet."

95 "I've never met him/her before in my life."

94 "She looked just like my Auntie Marjorie."

93 "I thought today was Monday."

92 "I've been offered a job in Saudi Arabia."

91 "I can't, it's half-term."

90 "If you'd been here on time this would never have happened."

89 "The Department of Trade withdrew their support."

88 "My knicker elastic broke."

87 "My fly broke, I couldn't help it."

86 "I can't, I'm allergic to horses."

85 "I'm not on the pill."

84 "Washing-up liquid brings me out in a rash."

83 "Mother needs me desperately."

82 "I spilt some super glue and I couldn't move."

81 "I didn't realise it was radio active."

80 "Didn't you feel the earth tremor just then?"

79 "The bus didn't come."

78 "There was a queue for the loo."

77 "I couldn't find a screw."

76 "I don't have the right hammer."

75 "It's not what you think, he mistook me for someone else."

74 "I must have grabbed hold of someone else's by mistake."

73 "Sorry, I haven't got my glasses."

72 "I can't until I've found my contact lens."

71 "I trod in a cow pat and had to go home to change my shoes."

70 "He/she was desperate, I had to stop and help."

69 "I think it must have been stolen."

68 "I mistook you for a kerb crawler."

67 "I thought you were about to attack me, so I kneed you in the groin."

66 "The post was late."

65 "There was fog on the A12."

64 "They'd sold the last one."

63 "They don't make it in puce."

62 "I think my back's gone again."

61 "It's against the law."

60 "When you've seen one you've seen them all."

59 "I didn't want to win anyway."

58 "It's the wrong time of the month."

57 "It must have had a leak in it."

56 "It just got too big for me to hold."

55 "I ran out of cream."

54 "We both got locked in."

53 "She's touring Australia."

52 "His grandmother's fallen down the cellar steps."

51 "It was raining."

50 "The chemist was closed."

49 "They threatened to call the police."

48 "We've all got food poisoning."

47 "Don't light up, there's a gas leak."

46 "The springs were rusty."

45 "I couldn't get it in."

44 "I forgot my cheque book."

43 "There's someone at the door."

42 "But my third wife wants me back."

41 "You know I can never do it on a Wednesday."

40 "It was only a small one, just to be sociable."

39 "I had no idea it was alcoholic."

38 "I had my back to him."

37 "I only did it to add spice to our marriage."

36 "Let's do it for the sake of the children."

35 "I only did it for you."

34 "I didn't know it was my turn."

33 "Nobody's ever shown me how."

32 "I'm not familiar with your equipment."

31 "I mistook it for the joy stick."

30 "I didn't think anyone would notice."

29 "I thought it was the Gents."

28 "I was only tying up my shoe laces."

27 "I couldn't read your handwriting."

26 "She was just showing me the correct position."

25 "I didn't realise it was strychnine."

24 "But you said that you would do it."

23 "I thought it would fit in, I measured it."

22 "The shop gave you the wrong size."

21 "We were in the dark because I was changing the film in her camera. I hope something develops."

20 "The hinges were rusty."

19 "I was just changing my trousers."

18 "I thought he was dead."

17 "It should look like that."

16 "It must have the wrong label on it."

15 "It's more than my job's worth."

14 "It just slipped out."

13 "I had my bifocals on by mistake."

12 "Sorry, I thought you said punt."

11 "Fanella's got the mumps."

10 "I was only giving her the benefit of my experience."

9 "I should never have had three helpings of curry."

8 "It's these Hay Fever tablets, I don't know what I'm doing."

7 "The baby sitter's got syphilis again."

6 "I've got poison ivy rash, just something that's going around."

5 "The knife slipped."

4 "The battery was flat."

3 "He needed comforting. His pet rat just died of the plague."

2 "I didn't know what to send a sick florist."

1 "Nobody told me!"

SOLID AND LASTING PEACE

Excuses to explain Divorce

"The only solid and lasting peace between a man and his wife is, doubtless, a separation."

LORD CHESTERFIELD

The ever increasing divorce rate today clearly proves that a great number of men and women who say 'I do', obviously don't. Many modern marriage ceremonies now omit the word 'obey', but a more realistic adjustment could be 'until divorce us do part'. The eighteenth century philosopher and satirist, Voltaire, claimed that divorce was invented two weeks after the first marriage, yet people still discuss separation in the same hushed tones that one would mention criminal abortion.

In Morocco a husband can divorce his wife simply by saying 'I divorce thee' three times. In England it's agony versus alimony, and excuses all the way to the divorce court. A young secretary being cited as co-respondent in a divorce case was questioned by the judge in court.

'Do you admit, Miss Ramsbottom, that you actually stayed in a hotel with this man?'

'Yes, I do, but he deceived me.'

'How did he do that?'

'He told the receptionist that I was his wife . . .'

Marriages may be 'made in Heaven', it's after the reception that they veer off towards Hell. Then it's excuses all the way! When living together finally becomes intolerable, most couples attempt a trial separation, but friends and family must never know:

1 "Bill's gone abroad on business."

2 "She's taken the children on a cruise."

3 "He's in quarantine."

4 "She's been nicked for shoplifting again, didn't you know?"

5 "He's had one of his little breakdowns, he's schizophrenic you know."

6 "She's on a course for six months. Suddenly decided that she wanted to be a ship welder."

7 "He's gone to have cosmetic surgery. He always was obsessed by the size of it."

8 "She's gone to a health farm for three months. I got rid of 150 lb of ugly fat the minute she went!"

9 "She couldn't bear the thought of the kids leaving home, so she's gone to university with Sally."

10 "He's writing a book about anacondas, had to go to Sri Lanka to study their eating habits."

Any excuse that encourages sympathy towards you, but gives no hint that your marriage might have failed! When eventually the 'split' becomes common knowledge, you must retain the sympathy at all costs. A marriage breakdown is never your fault:

1 "She drank."

2 "It was an incestuous relationship with his brother."

3 "She was frigid."

4 "He was having an affair with the Lady Mayoress, how can I possibly stand for council re-election?"

5 "She was having an affair, I should have realised when we moved from London to Edinburgh and still had the same milkman."

6 "He gambled all mother's inheritance."

7 "I was a battered husband."

8 "He was kinky, he used to like to tie me up. Then leave me for a fortnight."

9 "She was more interested in her knitting machine."

10 "He was working abroad so often that the kids forgot what he looked like!"

It's when you finally reach the divorce court that the excuses really fly thick and fast:

1 "I didn't realise he was a burglar, I turned over in bed and thought it was my husband. Yes, it did happen on ten separate occasions, but they look so much alike in the dark."

2 "My secretary used to be a Samaritan and we simply used to go for weekends in the country to discuss my problems."

3 "He became a member of this weird religious sect. I tried to be tolerant, but I drew the line at ritual sacrifice."

4 "She objected to me going to a massage parlour for my physiotherapy. Soho just happened to be convenient for the office."

5 "He was too casual about his appearance, sometimes I didn't see him for a fortnight."

6 "Her behaviour was unreasonable, she objected when I brought my work home. Yes, I do work in sewerage . . ."

7 "He's a pathologist, and he would keep trying to perform an autopsy on me in bed."

8 "She couldn't achieve an orgasm if I didn't hit her."

9 "He's the most selfish man I know, he's never brought diamonds or furs in twenty years of marriage. My best frock is still the one I wore to get married in."

10 "She only married me to try and get tax relief on her personal fortune."

Few would expect the Bible to condone divorce, yet in Proverbs it says quite clearly, 'It is better to dwell in the corner of the housetop, than with a brawling woman in a wide house.' Just help me up on to the roof . . .

SHOULD AULD ACQUAINTANCE BE FORGOT

Excuses for friends (and enemies!)

"Should auld acquaintance be forgot, and never brought to min'?"
ROBERT BURNS

Isn't it always when you're looking your absolute worst that you bump into people that you haven't clapped eyes on for years! Usually it's the very last person in the world that you want to see. In an eighteen-year old coat and looking like the Creature from the Black Lagoon, you've probably just popped out for a pound of sprouts and your valium prescription, when someon cries:

'It can't be! It *is* you! I'd recognise that walk anywhere!' and a ghost from the past steps up, dressed by Yves Saint Laurent with a Claude Montana jacket hung casually around their shoulders.

'What a surprise!' you smile through gritted teeth,

knowing only too well that you were wearing the same coat when you last met thirteen years ago.

Old friends have a habit of cropping up at the most inopportune moments. You are just coming out of the 'Special Clinic' or a discreet shop that sells marital aids; you are on your way *to* the hairdressers, or are queuing up at the chemists with an economy size pot of anti-wrinkle cream. There are some people who could walk back into your life at any time, and it would still be wrong! Fortunately our mouths and our minds are so well co-ordinated that we never say what we are actually thinking . . .

Mouth: "How lovely to see you again."
Mind: "I've managed to avoid you for years."

Mouth: "I lost your address."
Mind: "I threw it away."

Mouth: "We moved out of the area."
Mind: "We didn't want you to know where we were going."

Mouth: "You really haven't changed a bit."
Mind: "Just as obnoxious as you always were."

Mouth: "You really do look just the same."
Mind: "You always did look old for your age."

Mouth: "I'll tell the wife, she'll be so sorry she missed you."
Mind: "She'll be absolutely delighted."

Mouth: "My husband isn't with me at the moment."
Mind: "He's still hiding behind that parked car."

Mouth: "You must come over and have dinner some time."
Mind: "Not if we can help it."

Mouth: "If you're ever in the area do give us a ring."
Mind: "We can make sure we're out when you call round."

Mouth: "I'm so glad that you've done so well for yourself."
Mind: "I'm as jealous as hell."

Mouth: "Does your wife take an active part in your career?"
Mind: "Didn't you marry the Managing Director's daughter?"

Mouth: "Let's not leave it so long next time."
Mind: "Let's meet in twelve years time instead of thirteen."

Mouth: "Drop us a line and let us know your Norfolk
address."
Mind: "It will remind us never to take a holiday in Norfolk."

Before an opportunity arises to renew the acquaintance any
further, you must always be in a hurry:

1 "I've got to pick the children up from school."

2 "I was due at the dentist ten minutes ago."

3 "My car's on a meter, must get back before I get a ticket."

4 "It'll be another 50p at the car park if I don't rush back."

5 "My train goes in five minutes and I've got to get a ticket."

6 "We've got guests for lunch, I only popped out for some
tonics."

7 "Mustn't hold you up any longer."

8 "There's my probation officer, must hide."

IF IT WASN'T FOR THE 'OUSES IN BETWEEN

Estate Agent Excuses

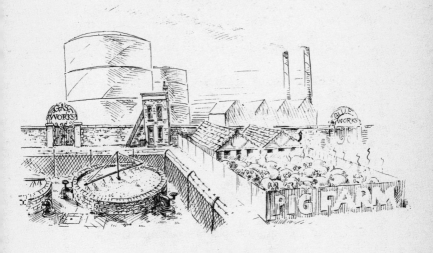

> *"Wiv a ladder and some glasses,*
> *You could see to 'Ackney Marshes,*
> *If it wasn't for the 'ouses inbetween."*
> **EDGAR BATEMAN**

Estate agents are of the same breed as salesmen, they will try and sell you anything to get the highest possible commission. In a speech, Prime Minister Benjamin Disraeli said: 'It is well known what a middle man is; he is a man who bamboozles one party and plunders the other.' To avoid being bamboozled or plundered, insist on having your own way. Don't be pressurised into buying a penthouse suite when you only intended to purchase a one-bedroomed flat.

'Yes, we do have something for £12,000,' they sneer, 'Shall we drive out and see if it's still standing?'

Yet, should it be a property that will not sell, they will use every excuse to bring its charms to your attention.

'There are a couple of slight disadvantages with this property; on the North is the sewerage, to the South are the gas works, on the West a glue factory, and in the East is a pig farm, BUT it is in your price range and you can always tell which direction the wind is blowing from.'

Before you study the property guide, and arrange the mortgage, have a survey done on your estate agent, or you may live in something you regret.

Excuse "I'm not sure that we have a property in your particular price range."
The Truth "You will never get a house for that price."

Excuse "The house does need some modest alterations."
The Truth "It needs completely redecorating, re-wiring and central heating put in."

Excuse "This house is in the heart of the countryside."
The Truth "There is a tree in the front garden, what more do you want?"

Excuse "The previous occupants are emigrating to Australia."
The Truth "They couldn't afford the rates."

Excuse "This delightful property is particularly inexpensive."
The Truth "They are going to build a motorway through it in five years time."

Excuse "The house is so handy for the trains."
The Truth "The line runs through your back garden."

Excuse "Within walking distance of the shops."
The Truth "Only if you're an olympic athlete."

Excuse "Easy access to the bus stop."
The Truth "It is only a five minute drive to the bus stop."

Excuse "This is a four-bedroomed house."
The Truth "If you don't have a lounge or dining-room you can have four bedrooms."

Excuse "There is a utility room."
The Truth "There is a shed at the side."

Excuse "The house has a delightful conservatory."
The Truth "There is a greenhouse attached."

Excuse "The property has all the charm of a country residence."
The Truth "There is no water, electricity or gas."

Excuse "We will advertise your house in the National press."
The Truth "We'll put an ad. in the local paper."

Excuse "The price of the property has gone up marginally."
The Truth "We've added another nought."

Excuse "The residence is most convenient for the airport."
The Truth "Concorde flies over every five minutes."

A guided tour of any property will result in more cracks from the estate agent than you will ever find in the ceiling:

Is that a damp patch in the ceiling?
"No, it's part of the pattern in the paper."

Surely that's a patch of dry rot on the floor?
"No, that mark is the bloodstain of Nelson. The floorboard actually came from the 'Victory', it is a great feature of the house."

The skirting board is loose.
"That's a secret panel for hiding papers behind."

There's a cockroach in the kitchen.
"The previous owner kept them as pets, that's the one that escaped. You know how attached animals become to their homes."

The wallpaper's peeling off the wall in the second bedroom.
"It's the re-usable kind. The owners are taking it with them."

The window frames have warped.
"Old houses have so much character, don't you think?"

The kitchen smells musty.
"Just Mrs Boswell's curry lingering in the air."

143

There's a terrific draught in the bedroom.
"It's the air-conditioning, it must be set for Summer."

The plaster appears to be crumbling.
"The surveyor took a little piece away, it will be repaired in
no time."

The wiring looks a bit ancient.
"It was all new last year, but was made to blend in with the
character of the house."

There's a fungus on the wall.
"The owner is a botanist, he likes to display rare plants."

This wall is terribly thin.
"That's not a wall, it's a window."

AS I WAS SAYING THE OTHER DAY

Intellectual Excuses

"As I was saying the other day . . ."

LUIS DE LÉON (Resuming a lecture after having been imprisoned for five years.)

Every day is the dawn of a new error. Appearing intellectual is not simply a matter of knowing the Theory of Relativity (Where there's a will there's a begging relative), being *au fait* with the works of Brecht, spotting the difference between art nouveau and art deco, or being able to hum highlights from Wagner's 'The Ring of the Nibelungs'. It is being able to hold your own with other so-called intellectuals who are frequently revealed to be pretentious snobs anyway! With a few well chosen excuses up your sleeve, you can appear as intelligent and as well educated as the next man. 'There is nothing stupid,' wrote Will Rogers, 'as an educated man, if you get off the thing that he was educated in."

The first question intellectuals will always ask is about your background:

Excuse "I was educated at Cambridge."
The Truth "I went to a primary school there."

Excuse "We always spend Christmas at Windsor."
The Truth "My sister Noreen has a flat there."

Excuse "We go down to Daddy's country estate most weekends."
The Truth "He's got a little market garden just outside Watford."

Excuse "We've traced my ancestry back to William the Conqueror."
The Truth "One of my ancestors must have been around in 1066."

Excuse "My wife went to a top girl's school."
The Truth "It was the local High."

Excuse "The Queen once said to me . . ."
The Truth "She definitely mentioned in her Christmas broadcast . . ."

Excuse "I have a private income."
The Truth "I claim Social Security."

Excuse "I work for the Government."
The Truth "All the money I pay in taxes must go somewhere."

Excuse "My wife's parents go to the Palace frequently."
The Truth "They always enjoy the cinema."

Making excuses to cover up your comprehensive school education, the fact that your mother's being detained to give Her Majesty Pleasure, and the reason why you haven't been employed since the winter of 1957, is simple when compared to being asked an outright question that you simply do not understand. To evade the issue say:

1 "Now that's a very controversial subject. What do *you* think?"

2 "Don't start me off on that subject, I could give you a whole dissertation on the matter."

3 "I never discuss politics."

4 "I work for the Foreign Office, I'm not allowed to go into things like that."

5 "I can't say, not since I signed the Official Secrets Act."

6 "Now that's something my wife is very keen on, tell him, dear."

7 "I can't bore you with my views, but you're the authority I would love to know about your views."

8 "I'm not sure how to take that, can you re-phrase the question."

9 "My goodness, is that the time? We must discuss this at some future date."

10 "I forget, it's years since I did my degree."

A highbrow is the kind of person who looks at a dish of coleslaw and thinks of Picasso. Trying to appreciate the works of modern artists when they look more like an accident on canvas can be very difficult. Even worse when it is a contemporary artist who can actually ask for your opinion about 'Brainstorm', two red splodges on a pink background, or some equally riveting masterpiece, which for £3500 you could have the pleasure of living with for the rest of your life. Having had my portrait painted twice, I know how embarrassing this can be, especially as in one I looked like Old Mother Riley. John Sargent said: 'Every time I paint a portrait I lose a friend.' Moral: never let a friend paint your portrait!

Frequently we would like to express what we really feel about modern art, but that would not appear intellectual. So, instead we make a meaningful comment . . .

Excuse "This work has childlike simplicity."
The Truth "It looks very childish."

Excuse "Very subtle brush technique."
The Truth "So subtle you'd think a four year old had done it."

Excuse "It would go well in my sister's drawing-room."
The Truth "My sister has impeccably bad taste."

Excuse "It must be wonderful to be so talented."
The Truth "To be paid so much for doing so little."

Excuse "I like the unusual angle from which the artist has chosen to paint his subject."
The Truth "Are you sure it isn't hanging upside-down?"

Excuse "It is most original."
The Truth "I have *never* seen anything like it!"

Excuse "Yes, it is mildly erotic."
The Truth "It's downright obscene."

Excuse "It grows on you."
The Truth "If it's going to increase in value, I could learn to live with it."

FATE CHOOSES YOUR RELATIONS

Excuses for and on behalf of your Family

"Le sort fait les parents, la choix fait les amis.
You choose your friends, fate chooses your relations."
ABBÉ JACQUES DELILLE

Blood may be thicker than water, but when you look at your relations it is so much more tempting to spill. Marriage contracts can be cancelled, lovers ditched, friends ostracised, but like it or not destiny deals you your relations, and you go through life clinging to a group of people whom you would probably never associate with through choice. The neurotic mother, work-shy father, dipsomaniac sister, glue-sniffing brother, all build up that rich tapestry called 'the family' and whatever your lot, you go through life accounting *for* them and *to* them. The only consolation is that you can never be blamed for your relations!

However bad they may seem, few of us would ever change them. Perhaps better the devils you know, but I suspect that thickness of the blood makes all the difference. Strange how some people are never quite happy with the colour of it though.

'I didn't ask to be born a Princess!' snapped Princess Anne in an interview just before her wedding, and to prove it she married a 'commoner' so that she could have untitled children. Ah, the other man's grass is always greener.

'Accidents will happen in the best regulated families,' wrote Charles Dickens, and because we accept our kith and kin for what they are, we make allowances for them too. There may be times when we deplore our family, but who amongst us would not defend them to the death . . .

Excuse "My brother is emotionally disadvantaged."
The Truth "He is as mad as a hatter."

Excuse "My sister just has a very full social life, that's all."
The Truth "The little tart's out with a different bloke every night."

Excuse "Mother has an alcohol problem."
The Truth "She can't stop drinking it."

Excuse "My father takes great pride in his work, and often stays late at the office."
The Truth "He's got a glamorous secretary, but that's his affair."

Excuse "My son works in computers."
The Truth "He screws the wheels on the bottom."

Excuse "My daughter is still pursuing her education."
The Truth "She's behind the bar in a working men's club."

Excuse "My father died before I was born."
The Truth "Shame it was before they had time to marry."

Excuse "Grandfather leads a very active life."
The Truth "He's a dirty old man."

Excuse "Grandma's very sprightly, always game for anything."

The Truth "She ought to be ashamed of herself, at her age!"

When you get married, not only does your family increase, but you gain a whole new set of relations. You may choose your spouse, but you can have no control over his or her relatives. I suppose visiting them relieves the monogamy, but as a friend of mine once remarked when gazing wistfully at a photograph of his mother-in-law, 'you know, Mother Nature can be a bitch!' Visits to in-laws can be kept to the bare minimum when you have excuses, excuses . . .

1   "But it's only two years since we last went there."

2   "We can't go, I haven't got the garlic and a crucifix."

3   "But you know the children have nightmares when they see anything nasty."

4   "I can't go without a present, and you can't get hemlock on a Sunday."

5   "You know I always come out in a rash when I kiss your mother."

6   "I'm allergic to your mother's poodle."

7   "There are much more important things to do; I'll mend the roof and decorate the stairs, weed the garden . . . anything."

8   "I'm sure you'd much prefer to visit your family on your own and have a good old natter."

9   "But it's fifty miles to your parent's house. Let's just drive to the zoo, it's cheaper."

10 "I can't possibly go, she's never liked me since I offered to donate her to Age Concern."

Mother-in-laws always come in for a lot of knocking, but when they will insist upon coming with you on the honeymoon, pay you one visit a year that lasts eleven months, and insist that their beloved child could have married better, it's little wonder. My poor father has a mother-in-law with a twin sister! Only Adam struck lucky when marrying Eve; neither of them had mothers and they were in Paradise!

'Are you a friend of the groom?' asked an usher at a wedding.

'Certainly not! I'm the bride's mother.'

The boot, however, is firmly on the other foot when your son or daughter falls in love with someone quite unsuitable.

It's not that I disapprove, dear, but:

1 "Why don't you at least wait until you're sixteen before you get married?"

2 "Her father's a tax inspector, you'd never have any money."

3 "He won't keep you in the style to which you've become accustomed on Social Security."

4 "She's almost as old as your mother!"

5 "Your children might end up having green hair too."

6 "I'm sure I read somewhere that there's lunacy in her family."

7 "He's too short. Your wedding photos will look ridiculous."

8 "Your mother would prefer you to wait."

9 "I don't think you'd like being a vicar's wife."

10 "She's only interested in that fifty thousand you won on the pools."

Although we can never see it, parents only advise us to do what they think is best. 'It's for your own good,' they cry from the time they try to bundle you into bed early at eight, and then stop you getting into bed early when you're eighteen! Odd how if you are successful it's put down to heredity and if you fail it's your own fault!

1 "She's passed her exams. Obviously gets it from me. I

would have got a degree if I hadn't left school at 13."

2 "He's failed. He gets his laziness from you!"

3 "She's decided to be a nurse. I was so right to let her play with that box of suppositories when she was seven."

4 "Malcolm's decided to have a year off to *prepare* for University."

5 "My son's not homosexual, he's just sensitive."

6 "Marilyn isn't promiscuous. She just enjoys her men friends."

7 "Our daughter does *not* work in a lavatory. She is a Convenience Superintendent." (Said proudly when your daughter *does* work in a public lavatory.)

8 "My Keith is a Water Systems Technician." (When your son is a plumber.)

EXCUSE ME, PRAY
The Ultimate Test

> *"Excuse me, pray."* Without that excuse I would not have known there was anything amiss.
>
> BLAISE PASCAL

Yes, we often make excuses when they are not even necessary. On a trip to Africa, Her Majesty the Queen was being driven in a horse-drawn carriage by the country's leader when loudly and explosively one of the horses broke wind.

'I'm so sorry,' said the Queen apologetically.

'Don't worry,' answered the African leader, 'if you hadn't said anything, I'd have thought it was the horse.'

Take a tip from the Queen and never apologise or make excuses unless you are absolutely forced.

As the ultimate test of your skill at making excuses here are twelve possible situations that you might get into, but how would you get out of them?

1 Whilst visiting a very rich friend, you accidentally smash a valuable Spode ornament. Do you say:

a) Sorry, I'll pay for it.
b) The cat brushed past it.
c) What a stupid place to stand it!

2 You put salt in the custard instead of sugar. Do you say:

a) My glasses were steamed up.
b) I'll make some more.
c) If you'd built that shelf like I asked, the sugar would have been to hand.

3 Your partner walks into a room and finds you half naked with a member of the opposite sex. Do you say:

a) I was just showing her my appendix scar.
b) Trust you to come in at the wrong moment.
c) I couldn't bear the heat in here.

4 Your partner arrives home unexpectedly and discovers you *in flagrante delicto*. Do you say:

a) It won't happen again.
b) This is Nurse Goodbody, she's just manipulating me.
c) If you haven't got something in the home, you have to go out for it!

5 Your children discover a copy of 'Playboy' in the bedroom. Do you say:

a) That's Daddy's, put it down!
b) So that's where I put my mail order catalogue.
c) It's a new biology book, you'll learn all about it one day.

6 You leave your wedding ring in someone else's house. Your husband notices the bare space on your finger. Do you say:

a) I'm having it made slightly larger.
b) I lent it to a friend.
c) I'm having it valued, in case we get a divorce.

7 You arrive home late, having had one drink too many. Do you say:

a) I thought rum and pep was a type of Cola.
b) I was only being sociable.
c) I was drinking to your health.

8 After a slight indiscretion you catch a minor infection and are forbidden sex for ten days. Do you say:

a) I caught something from the squash club showers.
b) This headache is going on for days.
c) Let's try separate rooms for fun.

9 Your partner discovers a Pools coupon in your pocket, not knowing that you've been doing them since 1965. Do you say:

a) Your mother asked me to post it.
b) I was going to try and win something as a surprise. Look, it's in your name.
c) But everybody does it.

10 You inadvertently have an item in your shopping bag which you haven't paid for. Do you say:

a) Someone obviously planted it there.
b) I thought they were a free sample.
c) Silly me! I picked up two by mistake.

11 Having told a friend that you will be out all evening, they drive by and see that you are in. Do you say:

a) A last minute change of plan!
b) The car wouldn't start.
c) I got my dates wrong, it's tomorrow!

12 The Inland Revenue discover that you have omitted a source of income from your Tax Return. Do you plead:

a) I must have missed that bit out.
b) It's such a small amount, I didn't think it counted.
c) That's my accountant's responsibility, not mine.

Now, what excuses have you made! Award yourself the following points:

1	a–0	b–10	c–5
2	a–5	b–0	c–10
3	a–10	b–0	c–5
4	a–0	b–10	c–5
5	a–0	b–10	c–5
6	a–10	b–0	c–5
7	a–10	b–5	c–0
8	a–10	b–5	c–0
9	a–5	b–10	c–0
10	a–0	b–10	c–5
11	a–0	b–5	c–10
12	a–0	b–5	c–10

Analysis

Score 0–35 What a goody-goody! You tell the truth so often that you could qualify for the *Guinness Book of Records*. Didn't they teach you anything at the convent?

35–75 You're a bit of a rogue on the quiet! You've not quite mastered the art of making excuses, but the potential is there. It's purely lack of confidence. The fear of being found out keeps you basically on the straight and narrow.

75–100 You will do anything to save your own skin, even if it means being deliberately deceitful. You are rarely in the wrong, because you can talk your way out of anything.

100–120 You tell enough white lies to ice a Christmas cake! There are no depths to which you will not sink to keep your reputation. "Attack is the best form of defence" is certainly your motto, and you would blame your own grandmother if you thought it would get you off the hook!

OTHER HUMOROUS BOOKS FROM RAVETTE

The Official British Yuppie Handbook The State-of-the Art Manual for Young Urban Professionals by Russell Ash
£2.50

Garfield

No. 1	Garfield The Great Lover	£1.25
No. 2	Garfield Why Do You Hate Mondays?	£1.25
No. 3	Garfield Does Pooky Need You?	£1.25
No. 4	Garfield Admit It, Odies's OK!	£1.25
No. 5	Garfield Two's Company	£1.25
No. 6	Garfield What's Cooking?	£1.25
No. 7	Garfield Who's Talking?	£1.25
No. 8	Garfield Strikes Again	£1.25
No. 9	Garfield Here's Looking At You	£1.25
No.10	Garfield We Love You Too	£1.25

Golfermania a light hearted look at the game of golf with cartoons by Qvist
£1.95

Howlers hilarious howlers of schoolchildren by Russell Ash
£1.95

All these books are available at your local bookshop or newsagent, or can be ordered direct from the publisher. Just tick the titles you require and fill in the form below. Prices and availability subject to change without notice.

Ravette Limited 12 Star Road, Partridge Green, Horsham, West Sussex RH13 8RA

Please send cheque or postal order, and allow the following for postage and packing.

Garfield: UK, Price 45p for one book, plus 20p for the second and 14p for each additional book ordered up to a £1.63 maximum.

Golfermania: Add 30p postage and packing.
Yuppie Handbook and Howlers: Add 45p postage and packing.

Name ....

Address ....

....